English Out There

Functional English and Life Skills

John Bryson
Dot Weaver

Hodder & Stoughton

LONDON SYDNEY AUCKLAND TORONTO

Acknowledgements

The publishers would like to thank the following for permission to reproduce their copyright material:

Alba Data Supplies; Alpha Key Communications Ltd; C E Barnes Ltd; Bramble Business Systems Ltd; British Elecrotechnical Approvals Board; British Gas; British Standards Institution; British Telecom; The Design Council; English Tourist Board; Fiveways Motorcycles; Her Majesty's Stationery Office for Crown Copyright material which is used by permission of the Controller; The Home Laundering Consultative Council; Honda (UK) Limited; The H.P. Motor Policies at Lloyd's; International Wool Secretariat; Kingston upon Hull City Transport; MBS Alveronic Computers Ltd; Miles Kingsport; National Westminster Bank plc; The North Eastern Electricity Board; Paris Travel Service; Photo Trade Processing Ltd; Pulman Motorcycles; Royal Life Insurance Limited; Star Bikes; Trainlines of Britain and the Woolwich Equitable Building Society.

We have been unable to trace the publishers of the map on page 56.

The authors would like to thank Mr E Lund for valuable advice on Chapter 5.

British Library Cataloguing in Publication Data
Bryson, John
  English out there.
  1. English language—Grammar—1950—
  I. Title
  428   PE112

ISBN 0 7131 7477 3

First published 1986
© 1986 John Bryson and Dot Weaver
Third impression 1990

Printed in Great Britain for the educational publishing division of Hodder and Stoughton Ltd., Mill Road, Dunton Green, Sevenoaks, Kent by The Bath Press, Bath

Contents

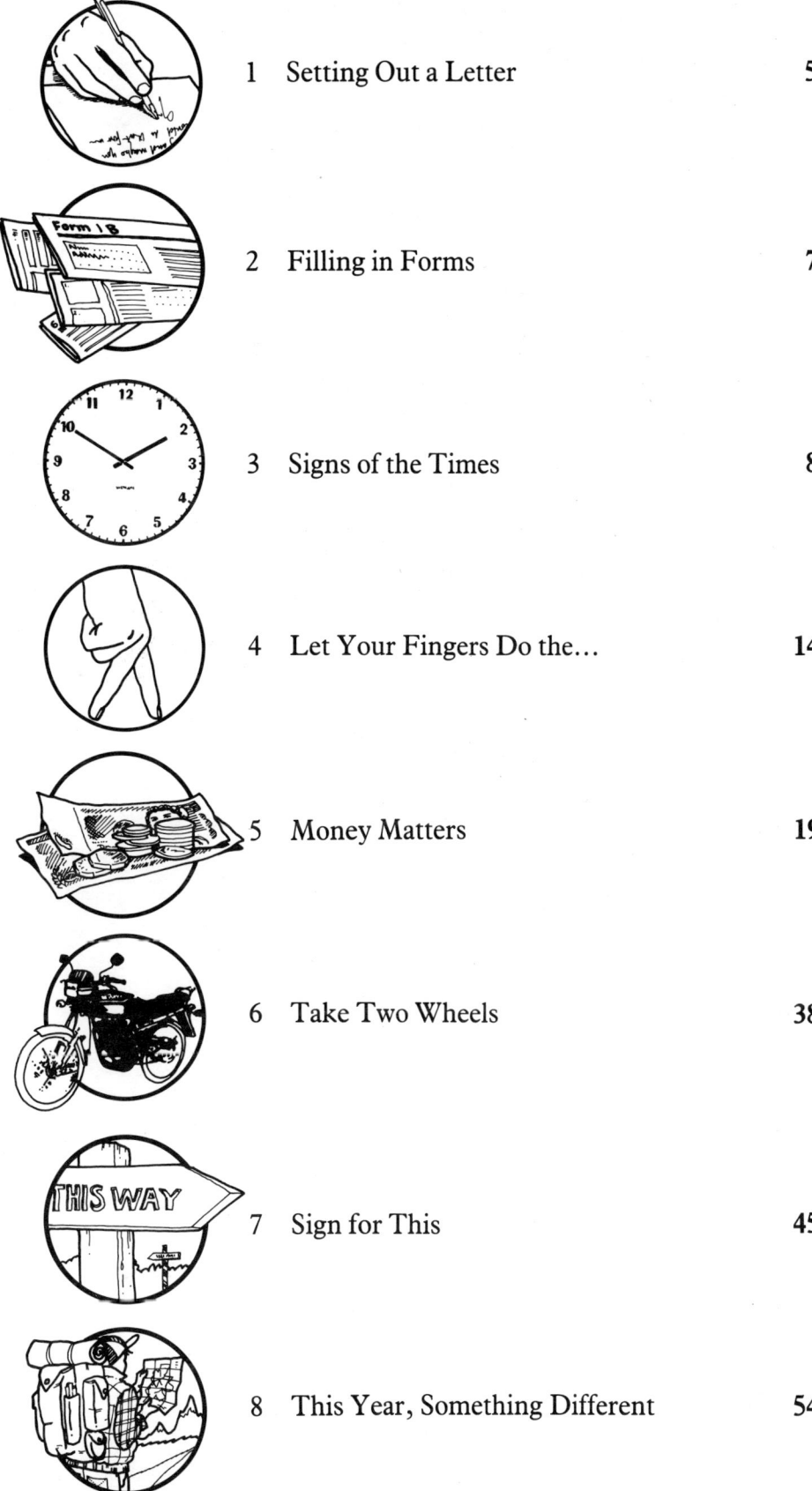

Preface

This book springs directly from our own teaching experience. We have called the book *English Out There* because, simply, that is what it concerns – English which is needed to follow everyday activities. We recognise that there is a need for practice in specific skills, and therefore our material is linked directly to the listening, speaking, reading and writing which pupils must master to satisfy their linguistic needs as young adults.

The purpose of this book is to provide a range of activities through which teachers can assist pupils to gain confidence and develop their ability to listen, talk, read and write effectively in real situations. The exercises allow them to tackle assignments individually, in pairs and in groups.

We feel that it is essential that these tasks should be completed whilst pupils can still receive professional guidance and encouragement. Our functional approach is not intended to diminish the importance of literature and creative work as the heart of English in the classroom, but to complement it.

John Bryson
Dot Weaver

1 Setting Out a Letter

Every letter needs:

1 the sender's address
2 the date
3 a greeting
4 an ending
5 the sender's signature

Here is the proper way to lay out a friendly or informal letter:

A business letter is any letter intended to promote business rather than friendship. Its range is, therefore, wide.

A business letter should be:

1 Brief   – businessmen are busy.
2 Clear   – be relevant.
3 Courteous – business letters are written to promote a particular line of business, politeness is an asset.

---

① { 33 Chestnut Road,
        Willerby,
        Hull.
           HU5 3BX
② { 24th March 1985

Dear John, } ③

Yours sincerely, } ④

Tom Brown } ⑤

---

                    33 Chestnut Road,
                    Willerby,
                    Hull.
                       HU5 3BX
                    29th March 1985

The Manager,
Supreme Plastics,
Bankside Industrial Est,
Hull,
HU13 2AC

Dear Sir,

              Yours faithfully,

              Tom Brown
              Tom Brown

Exercise 1

Write a letter to a friend who has moved away, inviting him or her to stay with you.

Envelopes may be addressed in either of these styles:

```
The Manager,
Supreme Plastics,
Bankside Industrial Estate,
Hull.
HU13 2AC
```

```
The Manager,
  Supreme Plastics,
    Bankside Industrial Estate,
      Hull.
        HU13 2AC
```

Exercise 2

Find the following addresses:

1 a local insurance broker
2 a trade union office
3 your M.P.

Address an envelope to each one.

Exercise 3

Look for a job advertisement in your local paper. Write a letter of application in response to the advertisement.

Remember
* Be careful with the layout.
* Your handwriting and spelling should be as good as you can make them.

Exercise 4

Work with a partner.
Imagine that you are penfriends. Write letters of introduction and then reply to your partner's letter.

A Letter of Complaint

A letter of complaint should be firm yet polite. Do be diplomatic.

Your Words	Diplomatic Language
I want	I would like
You are wrong	{ There seems to be a mistake / You appear to be mistaken
Immediately	{ At your convenience / As soon as possible / By return of post
I need	Can you supply?
I want this sorting out now!	{ Within seven days / My solicitors will be contacting you

Exercise 5

Write an answer to this letter of complaint:

```
                                    33 Chestnut Road,
                                       Willerby,
                                         Hull.
                                          HU5 3BX
                                    16th April 1985

The Manager,
Discs by Post,
P.O. Box 123,
Leeds.
LS1 6DQ

Dear Sir,
        It is over six weeks
since I sent for a set of four L.P.
'Chart Toppers' which you
advertised on television.

        You promised delivery
within 28 days. My records have
not arrived. I want my money back
or my records tomorrow.

        Yours faithfully,
        Tina Brown
        Tina Brown (Miss)
```

2 Filling in Forms

Remember
* ★ Always use a pen to complete a form.
* ★ Never use an erasable pen or pencil.
* ★ Read the form first. If there is anything which you do not understand ask a friend or relative for help. If there is a technical problem, ask a professional for assistance.

Here are some words and expressions found on many forms. Learn their meaning.

BLOCK CAPITALS PLEASE
COMPLETE IN BLOCK
CAPITALS } These all mean use capital letters
BLOCK CAPITALS
PRINT YOUR NAME

First
Fore } All of your names except your surname
Christian
Other

Surname   Your last name

Initials   The first letter of each of your names

Postal Address } The place to which
Full Address } letters should be sent

Delete   Cross out

Declaration   A statement that you have told the truth

Signature   Your name written in your usual way

D.O.B. } The date on which you
Date of Birth } were born

For Official Use
For Office Use } Do not write in any
For Company Use } such space
Do not write here

Application Form   *Do not write here*

Applicant _____
Surname _____
Forename(s) _____
Delete Mr/Mrs/Miss/Ms
Other titles _____
Permanent address in the U.K.

_____
_____
_____
_____

Post Code _____
D.O.B. _____

Declaration
I declare that I have checked the information given on this form and to the best of my knowledge it is correct.

Signed _____
Date _____

This form has to be completed by James Andrew Smith of 3 Camperdown Road, Beverley, North Humberside, HU13 3XY. He was born on 31st March 1962.

Exercise 6

Copy and complete the above form.

3 Signs of the Times

Your school will have a timetable. This will be a plan showing the work to be done, a place and a time for it. A timetable is needed to make sure that everyone gets to the correct place at the proper time.

Example
Here is a teacher's timetable. It shows who he teaches, where, when and for how long.

		MON	TUE	WED	THUR	FRI	
9:15							Registration 8:45 to 9:15
	1	5E6B 8	6V 14	6EA 14	Library	4E1B 14	
9:55	2	5E6B 8	6V 14	6EA 14	6E2E 13	4E1B 14	
10:30							10:30 to 10:45
	3	6E1E 11	5E6B 9		4E5A 14	5E6A 9	
11:20	4	6E1E 11	5E6B 9		4E1B 14	5E6B 9	
11:55							Lunch until 1:15
	5	4E1B 14		4E5A 14		6EA 14	
2:00	6	4E1B 14		4E5A 14		6EA 14	
2:35	7	5E6A 9	7EA 14	7EA 14	5E6A 14	4E5A 14	
3:10	8	5E6A 9	7EA 14	7EA 14	5E6A 14	4E5A 14	
3:45							

Exercise 7

a) Are all the lessons of equal length?
b) How long are most of the lessons?
c) In which room does the teacher spend most of his time?
d) How long is each school day?
e) How much preparation time does this teacher have?
f) On which day does he teach the most lessons?
g) How long is morning registration?
h) If a parent wanted to have a meeting with this teacher, when would be the best time?

Exercise 8

Have you ever misread your timetable and gone to the wrong classroom? Try to remember a time when you went to the wrong place. How did you feel? Where you very embarrassed? How did other people react to your mistake?

Write a story about someone who gets lost in school.

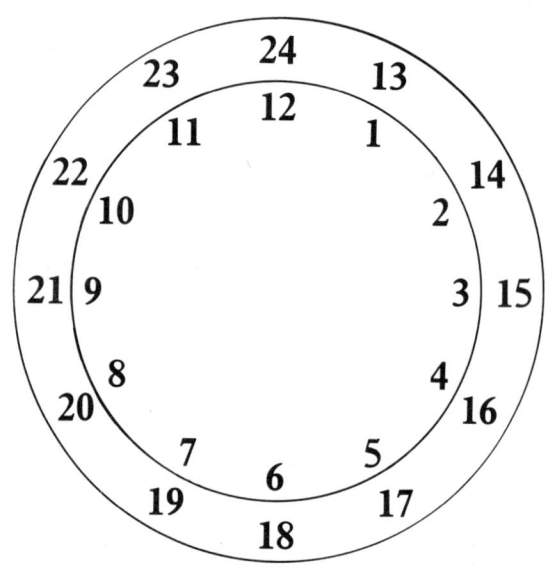

Most pupils use their school timetable very well. This is because they are used to it and know how it works.

Bus and train timetables are different. They may appear difficult to use – until you know how to read them.

These timetables use the 24-hour clock, which is shown in the drawing above. The first twelve hours from **1** to **12** are inside and the next twelve hours from **13** to **24 (00)** are outside.

The 24-hour clock does not run from **1** to **12** twice a day. It runs from **1** to **12** for the morning and begins the afternoon with **12+1** which is **13**.

Example
10.00a.m. is **1000** hours on the 24-hour clock.
 4.00p.m. is **1600** hours, that is **12+4 = 1600**.

Exercise 9

Write down these times, using the 24-hour clock:

a)   7.00a.m.   f)   5.20p.m.
b)   11.15a.m.   g)   7.32p.m.
c)   noon   h)   8.15p.m.
d)   1.45p.m.   i)   10.26p.m.
e)   3.17p.m.   j)   11.57p.m.

Exercise 10

Use the 24-hour clock and write down the times at which you:

a)   get up in the morning
b)   begin lessons at school
c)   end your morning break
d)   have lunch
e)   arrive home after school
f)   have tea
g)   watch your favourite television programme
h)   go to bed

Remember
★   there is no midnight or noon.
★   Midnight is called **0000** hours.
★   Noon is called **1200** hours.
★   Although we say fourteen hundred hours, there are only sixty minutes in each hour. So fourteen fifty-nine is followed by fifteen hundred hours.

Exercise 11

Draw one day from your school timetable and write in the lesson times using the 24-hour clock.

Exercise 12

Draw a 24-hour digital clock of your own. Write beside it the things you would do at the weekend or in the holidays.

24-hour Clock Search

Look for the following times amongst the figures in the square below.

five minutes past midday
quarter past ten in the morning
half past three in the afternoon
10.07 p.m.
five fifty-five a.m.
twenty minutes to midnight
one o'clock in the morning
nine nineteen a.m.
four minutes past four in the morning
four minutes past four in the afternoon
quarter past seven in the evening
6.28 p.m.
quarter to eleven a.m.
twenty past eight p.m.
ten to three in the afternoon
twelve minutes past three in the morning
nine minutes past eleven in the morning
two minutes to seven p.m.
five forty p.m.
one thirty-nine p.m.
six twenty-five a.m.
7.19 p.m.
thirteen minutes to four p.m.
2.54 p.m.

8	5	8	1	4	5	0	9	3	6
0	6	0	2	1	0	0	1	0	3
0	5	0	4	8	2	6	5	3	3
1	2	2	3	3	1	0	1	5	0
9	6	7	0	2	2	7	1	1	7
1	0	4	5	1	7	4	0	8	2
4	6	5	5	0	9	1	9	0	9
5	1	1	5	6	4	1	2	3	1
4	7	1	3	3	9	0	5	1	9
5	1	3	4	2	2	9	4	2	1

Train Guide

Railway stations display large timetables for travellers to read and issue pocket timetables for specific routes so that travellers can plan journeys efficiently.

Here is a map showing stations on the Hull to Sheffield line.

a) When does the first train leave Hull for Goole on August Bank Holiday?
b) At what time does the first train from Hull arrive at Gilberdyke?
c) Would a porter be available to help you with your luggage at Broomfleet?
d) Which station does not have a car park?
e) At what time does the first train for Sheffield leave Doncaster?
f) When does the first train leave Brough after 1600 hours on: Friday? Tuesday?
g) What is the shortest possible journey time between Sheffield and Doncaster?
h) How many trains run between Ferriby and Hull after 1700 hours on: Wednesday? Friday?

Exercise 13

a) Some stations are marked with a circle others by a square. Why is this?
b) Which are the Inter-City stations?
c) Why would an Inter-City train not stop at Gilberdyke?

Hull – Doncaster – Sheffield
Mondays to Saturdays

		▨②	②	▨②		②	②	②		②	②		②
Hull P	d.	0738	0749	–	0758	0820	0841	0854	–	0940	–	0953	–	10 14	–
Hessle P	d.	–	0757	–	08 06	–	–	–	–	–	–	–	10 22	–
Ferriby P	d.	–	08 03	–	08 12	–	–	–	–	–	–	–	10 28	–
Brough P	d.	0752	08 10	–	08 17	08 34	08 55	09 08	–	09 54	–	10 08	–	10 33	–
Broomfleet ‡ P	d.	–	08 17	–	08 24	–	–	–	–	–	–	–	10 40	–
Gilberdyke P	d.	–	08 22	–	08 29	–	09 05	–	–	–	–	–	10 45	–
Saltmarshe ‡ P	d.	–	08 28	–	–	–	–	–	–	–	–	–	10 51	–
Goole P	d.	–	0834a	–	08 51	–	–	–	1009	–	–	–	10 58	–
Thorne Nth. P	d.	–	–	–	09 01	–	–	–	–	–	–	–	11 08	–
Stainforth & H. P	d.	–	–	–	–	–	–	–	1014	–	–	11 15	–
Doncaster P	a.	–	–	–	08 17	–	–	–	1031	1027	–	11 27	–
Doncaster P	d.	–	–	09 05	09 33	–	10 04	–	1037	–	1105	11 31	1205
Conisbrough P	d.	–	–	09 14	09 42	–	1013	–	1046	–	1114	11 40	1214
Mexborough P	d.	–	–	09 19	09 47	–	1018	–	1051	–	1119	11 46	1219
Rotherham P	d.	–	–	09 30	1001	–	1029	–	1102	–	1130	11 57	1231
Attercliffe ‡	d.	–	–	–	–	–	–	–	–	–	–	–	–
Sheffield P	a.	–	–	0941	1012	–	1040	–	11 12	–	1141	12 09	1242

NOTES: ▨ Does not run Bank Holidays.   a – Arrival time.
P – Car parking facilities available.   ‡ – No staff in attendance.   ② – Second class only.

Here is a typical railway timetable. The stations are listed in the same order as they appear on the map. Departure times for each train are listed in order. The earliest is on the left.

Example
The first train from Hull departs at 0738 hours and goes straight to Brough, arriving at 0752 hours.

Exercise 14

Read the railway timetables and footnotes, then answer the questions.

Sheffield – Doncaster – Hull
Mondays to Saturdays

				②	F ②	②		②		▨②	②	②	G ②		②
Sheffield P	d.	–	1249	1325	–	1352	1419	–	–	14 45	–	1523	–	–	1554	–
Attercliffe ‡	d.	–	–	–	–	–	–	–	–	1452	–	1530	–	–	1601	–
Rotherham P	d.	–	1256	1332	–	1359	1426	–	–	1503	–	1541	–	–	16 12	–
Mexborough P	d.	–	1307	1344	–	14 11	1437	–	–	1508	–	15 46	–	–	–
Conisbrough P	d.	–	1312	1348	–	14 16	1442	–	–	1519	–	15 57	–	–	16 28	–
Doncaster P	a.	–	1324	1359	–	14 26	1453	–	–	1525	1536	–	16 13	–	16 35	–
Doncaster P	d.	–	13 28	–	1414	14 35	–	–	1546	–	16 24	–	–	–
Stainforth & H. P	d.	–	1339	–	–	14 46	–	–	1540	1552	–	16 30	–	1648	–
Thorne Nth. P	d.	–	1345	–	–	–	–	–	1551	1605	–	1642a	–	1700	1714
Goole P	d.	–	13 55	–	14 36	–	–	–	–	16 10	–	–	–	1719
Saltmarshe ‡ P	d.	–	–	–	–	–	–	15 55	–	16 17	–	–	–	1728
Gilberdyke P	d.	–	–	–	–	–	–	–	–	16 22	–	–	–	1731
Broomfleet ‡ P	d.	–	–	–	–	–	–	1602	1606	16 12	16 29	–	17 12	17 18	1737
Brough P	d.	1401	14 12	–	14 51	–	–	1607	–	16 38	–	1717	–	1745
Ferriby P	d.	–	–	–	–	–	–	16 12	–	16 41	–	17 22	–	1750
Hessle P	d.	–	–	–	15 06	–	–	16 20	16 24	16 28	16 52	–	1731	1735	1759
Hull P	a.	1421	1428	–	15 06	–	–	16 20	16 24	16 28	16 52	–	1731	1735	1759

NOTES: ▨ – Does not run Bank Holidays.   a – Arrival time.   P – Car parking facilities available.
F – Fridays only.   G – Mondays to Thursdays only.
‡ – No staff in attendance.   ② – Second class only.

i) At what time does the last train leave Broomfleet for Hull?
j) If you arrived at Sheffield at 1209 hours and spent three hours shopping, by which train could you return to Thorne Nth.?
k) How long is the last journey from Saltmarshe to Hessle?
l) Are there any first class seats on the 1325 hours from Sheffield?
m) How many trains from Sheffield call at Brough?

Station	Tel:	Open
Sheffield	Sheffield (0742) 26411	Daily 24 hours
Rotherham		
Mexborough		Weekdays 0800-2200
Conisbrough	Doncaster	Sundays 0900-2200
Doncaster	(0302) 20191	Weekdays 0900-1630
Stainforth &	Doncaster (0302) 841244	Weekdays 0600-2130
Hatfield		
Thorne North	Thorne (0405) 812137	Daily 0700-1900
Goole	Goole (0405) 3297	Sun. to Fri. 0800-2100
Hull, Brough	Hull (0482) 26033/4	Saturdays 0800-2000
Ferriby, Hessle		
Gilberdyke		

Exercise 15

a) Which information office is open all day?
b) Where can you reserve a seat?
c) Suggest a reason to explain why some of the information offices are open for longer hours than others.
d) How would you apply for a season ticket?

Bus Timetables and Faretables

This table tells travellers which bus route serves each area of the city:

INDEX OF PLACES SERVED
REFERENCES are to Service Numbers.
TIMETABLES and FARETABLES are arranged in numerical order of Service numbers.

SERVICES FROM THE CITY CENTRE

Destination (or place)	Service(s)
Anlaby Road	6, 60, 61, 63, 64, 67
Asda	56
Beverley Road	16, 17, 18, 30, 31
Bilton Grange	10, 48, 58
Bodmin Road	31, 35, 36
Boothferry Estate	6, 73
Boothferry Park	6, 67
Boulevard	6, 60, 61, 63, 64, 67
Bransholme	30,31,32,33,34,35,36,37,38,39
Bransholme District Centre	30, 31, 32, 33, 34, 35
Bransholme North	30, 32, 39
Bricknell Avenue	14, 15
Brunswick	16
Calvert Road	11, 60, 61, 64, 71, 72
Chanterlands Avenue	13, 15
Chestnut Farm	34
Cleveland Street	36, 37, 38, 39, 41
Clough Road	70
Compass Road	16
Cottingham Road	18
Cranbrook Avenue	20
Craven Park	34, 48, 55, 56, 58
Dairycoates	10, 11, 71, 72, 73, 75
Dansom Lane	33
Derringham Bank	1, 2, 3, 4, 75
Drypool	33, 43, 45
East Carr	34
East Hull Estate	43, 45
East Park	34, 48, 55, 56, 58

Example
If a traveller wanted to go to Bodmin Road there are three buses which would take him or her there, as the index shows:

Bodmin Road.............................31, 35, 36

Exercise 16

Write down the answers to these questions:

a) Which bus service goes to Asda?
b) Which service goes to Bricknell Avenue?
c) To which places does the service **48** go?
d) Where will the service **70** take you?

The following plan shows travellers where to find the departure stand they need:

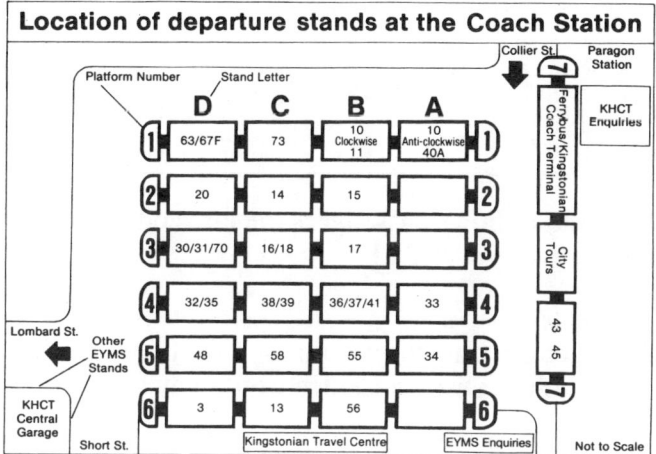

Example
A passenger wishing to travel to Bricknell Avenue would look at the **Index of Places Served**. This would tell him or her to use service **14** or **15**.

He or she would then look for the service numbers on the plan showing the **Location of Departure Stands**. Service **14** departs from platform **2** stand **C** and service **15** from platform **2** stand **B**. He or she could then choose to travel on whichever service was the most convenient.

Exercise 17

Write down the answers to these questions:

a) From which departure stand do the Beverley Road services operate?
b) Which services use departure stand **4B**?
c) For which service is platform **7** the departure point?
d) What is the destination of the service which uses stand **5A**?

Fare Code values	Adult	Child Scholar	Senior Citizen
A	10	10	10
B	15	10	10
C	20	10	10
D	25	10	10
E	30	10	10

There are five adult fare codes shown in the table above. Children, scholars and senior citizens pay a standard rate of ten pence per journey.

```
Stage
 1    COACH STATION                                                          FARES
 2    A    Norfolk Street                                                    Service
 3    B    A    St. Hilda Street                                               31
 4    C    B    A    Melwood Grove
 5    C    C    B    A    Haworth Street (or Cottingham Road Garage)
 6    C    C    C    B    A    Endike Lane
 7    C    C    C    C    B    A    Sutton Road/Ennerdale
 8    C    C    C    C    C    B    A    Cheltenham Avenue (Coleford Grove)
 9    D    D    D    C    C    C    A    A    Finningley Garth
10    D    D    D    D    C    C    A    A    A    Patrington Garth
11    D    D    D    D    C    C    A    A    A    BRANSHOLME (District Centre)
```

This table shows passengers the fare codes for journeys on service **31**.

Example
A passenger travelling from the Coach Station to Bransholme District Centre would pay fare **D**.

Exercise 18

a) Which is the fare code for a journey from the Coach Station to Endike Lane?
b) If a passenger got on the bus at Melwood Grove and paid fare **C**, to which places could he or she travel?
c) Where must a passenger get off the bus if he or she got on at Norfolk Street and paid a 15 pence fare?

Exercise 19

Read the timetable for service **31** and then answer the following questions:

a) When does the first bus leave Bransholme District Centre on: Monday? Sunday?
b) At what time does the next bus leave Bransholme District Centre after 1300 hours on: Saturday? Sunday?
c) When does the first bus leave the Coach Station on: Friday? Sunday?
d) How many buses leave the Coach Station for Bransholme District Centre between 1300 hours and 1500 hours on: Tuesday? Sunday?
e) After 1600 hours, when does the next bus leave Bransholme District Centre?
f) When does the last bus leave the Coach Station?
g) At what time does the last bus to Bransholme District Centre leave the Coach Station?
h) What is the destination of the 2235 hours bus from the Coach Station?
i) How often do the buses leave the Coach Station between:
0700 and 1100 hours on Monday?
1900 and 2130 hours on Friday?
1200 and 2000 hours on Sunday?
j) From which departure stand does the service **31** leave the coach station?
k) Which service goes to Bransholme, Bransholme District Centre and Bransholme North?

This timetable for the service 31 to Bransholme District centre uses the 24-hour clock.

COACH STATION : BRANSHOLME (District Centre)   Service **31**
via Beverley Road, Sutton Road, Ennerdale, Littondale, Cheltenham Avenue, Bude Road, Bodmin Road, Bude Road, Noddle Hill Way, Wawne Road, Barnstaple Road, Goodhart Road.

From COACH STATION			From BRANSHOLME (District Centre)		
Monday to Friday	Saturday	Sunday	Monday to Friday	Saturday	Sunday
—	—	—	06—18,38,58	06—18,38,58	06—45
07—10,30,50	07—10,30,50	—	07—18,38,58	07—18,38,58	07—45
08—10,30,50	08—10,30,50	08—00	08—18,38,58	08—18,38,58	08—45
09—10,30,50	09—10,30,50	09—00	09—18,38,58	09—18,38,58	09—45
10—10,30,50	10—10,30,50	10—00	10—18,38,58	10—18,38,58	10—45
11—10,30,50	11—10,30,50	11—00	11—18,38,58	11—18,38,58	11—45
12—10,30,50	12—10,30,50	12—00,30	12—18,38,58	12—18,38,58	12—45
13—10,30,50	13—10,30,50	13—00,30	13—18,38,58	13—18,38,58	13—15,45
14—10,30,50	14—10,30,50	14—00,30	14—18,38,58	14—18,38,58	14—15,45
15—10,30,50	15—10,30,50	15—00,30	15—18,38,58	15—18,38,58	15—15,45
16—10,30,50	16—10,30,50	16—00,30	16—18,38,58	16—18,38,58	16—15,45
17—10,30,50	17—10,30,50	17—00,30	17—18,38,58	17—18,38,58	17—15,45
18—10,30	18—10,30	18—00,30	18—18,38,58	18—18,38,58	18—15,45
19—00,30	19—00,30	19—00,30	19—15,45	19—15,45	19—15,45
20—00,30	20—00,30	20—00,30	20—15,45	20—15,45	20—15,45
21—00,30	21—00,30	21—00,30	21—15,45	21—15,45	21—15,45
22—00■,35■	22—00■,35■	22—00■,35■	22—15	22—15	22—15
23—00■	23—00■	23—00■	—	—	—

CODE   ■ Journey terminates at Barnstaple Road. Does **not** enter the District Centre.

Remember
* If a railway or bus timetable is set out in columns like the one on page 10 the journey begins at the top and ends at the bottom.
* If there is nothing printed next to a station or a stop, the train or bus does not stop.
* A timetable will have a fresh column for each new departure.
* Always read the notes very carefully.

Wordsearch

The words which follow can all be found in the wordsearch below. They may run in any direction. See if you can find them all.

Coach Station
Terminus
Passenger
Location
Arrival
Application
Senior Citizen
Departure
Traveller
Route
Adult
Reservation
Timetable
Platform

Porter
Service
Railway Station
Travel Centre
Inter-City
Luggage
Season Ticket
Board
Destination
Information
Journey
Scholar
Faretable
Alight

J	L	T	E	K	C	I	T	N	D	S	A	E	S	G	X	M	U	B
I	S	C	H	O	L	A	R	R	I	V	A	L	G	C	C	Q	D	U
P	E	C	I	V	R	E	S	Y	A	D	N	U	S	A	D	X	C	Q
G	N	O	I	T	A	T	S	H	C	A	O	C	T	H	G	I	L	A
F	I	N	N	R	O	R	Q	Y	R	I	I	B	R	N	R	G	Y	Y
T	O	C	F	A	D	E	U	D	E	R	T	E	R	M	I	N	U	S
F	R	H	O	V	T	T	X	C	S	X	A	L	N	F	N	D	L	L
W	C	A	R	E	R	R	F	D	E	S	T	I	N	A	T	I	O	N
P	I	Q	M	L	A	O	D	L	R	S	S	V	C	R	I	N	C	O
N	T	X	A	C	V	P	E	W	V	Q	Y	T	H	E	M	T	A	N
G	I	K	T	E	E	A	P	O	A	C	A	L	F	T	E	E	T	H
K	Z	I	I	N	L	S	A	L	T	P	W	U	F	A	T	R	I	Y
W	E	E	O	T	L	S	R	J	I	U	L	D	N	B	A	C	O	U
T	N	X	N	R	E	E	T	I	O	C	I	A	W	L	B	I	N	D
X	I	V	A	E	R	N	U	Q	N	U	A	E	T	E	L	T	H	P
X	Q	X	I	W	O	G	R	J	S	O	R	T	G	F	E	Y	H	C
B	X	H	I	V	U	E	E	T	E	Y	B	N	I	B	O	A	R	D
W	L	H	B	Q	T	R	W	G	A	E	V	P	E	O	X	R	L	Q
K	B	D	P	G	E	J	D	A	K	R	M	L	V	Y	N	E	M	E

Things to do

1 Make a collection of bus and train timetables. Find some services which operate from your town or area. Try to get:
   i   a local bus timetable
   ii a long distance coach timetable
   iii an Inter-City railway timetable
   iv a local or commuter timetable

2 Read your timetables and collect information about a particular route or destination. Prepare a short talk telling about your chosen route, you may like to include:
   i   earliest departures
   ii last evening departure
   iii quickest service
   iv stations or places served
   v   the train or bus which stops at the most places

3 Use your timetables to work out how to get to the following places   a) quickly b) cheaply:
   i   London
   ii Manchester
   iii Edinburgh
   iv a seaside resort

4 Find out the most convenient way to get to your nearest airport.

5 Try to find examples of other types of timetable. Look in a diary – most diaries have an underground railway map. Try to find an underground timetable.

6 Your school timetable will probably give you four pieces of information about any period or lesson:
   i   class
   ii classroom, laboratory or workshop
   iii teacher's name or initials
   iv subject

   What information will a bus timetable usually give you?

7 How many pieces of information does any of your railway timetables give you? List them.

4   Let Your Fingers do the...

A B C D E F G H I J K L M N O P Q R S T U V W X Y Z

Dictionaries list words in alpahabetical order. Words which begin with the letter **A** are listed first. A telephone directory lists its subscribers (the people who have telephones) in the same way. Names which begin with the letter **A** are listed first.

If you know a subscriber's surname you can start to find his or her telephone number.

Example
Here is a list of subscribers arranged in surname order:

Archer	(Notice that there is only one
Blake	name starting with **A** and three
Bones	with **B**. **Blake** is listed before
Budding	**Bones** and **Budding** as its
Carter	second letter **l** comes before **o**
Cunningham	and **u** in the alphabet.)
Day	
Dearness	
Dodsworth	

Exercise 20

Arrange these surnames in alphabetical order:

Peters	Robinson	Ratheram
Andrews	Adcock	Brown
Potter	Jones	Spence
Codd	Marrow	McDougall
Bright	Dobson	Evans

Most telephone directories have a lot of subscribers with the same surname. Brown, Jones, Robinson and Smith are common examples. To help users to find the number of the person they want to telephone, the directory lists entries with the same surname in alphabetical order of initials. A surname with the initial **A** is listed before those with initial **B**.

Example
The following list of subscribers called **Jones** is in alphabetical order of initials.

Jones P.H,	Jones P.H.K,	Jones P.M,
Jones P.H,	Jones P.J,	Jones P.M.O,
Jones P.H,	Jones P.J.K,	Jones P.N,
Jones P.H.J,	Jones P.K,	Jones P.N.B,

Exercise 21

Put this list of **Smiths** into the order in which you would find them in a directory.

Smith S,	Smith F,	Smith J.O,
Smith S.B.C,	Smith T.E,	Smith A,
Smith A.D,	Smith C.A,	Smith N,
Smith A.D.E,	Smith E.G,	Smith N.O,
Smith R,	Smith P.M,	Smith M,

When a group of subscribers have the same surname and initials they are listed in alphabetical order by their address.

Example
The subscribers listed below have the same surname and initials. See how they are listed.

Carr P.J,	49 Middlethorpe Avenue,
Carr P.J,	7 Nile Street,
Carr P.J,	39 Peel Street

Some of the entries in a telephone directory give the subscriber's occupation. This is usually abbreviated to save space.

Example

Ellis R, Photog,	– Photographer
Ellis R, Frmr,	– Farmer
Ellis R,	
Ellis R, Mtr Cycs,	– Motor Cycle Dealer
Ellis R, Nwsagt,	– Newsagent

Exercise 22

Copy these abbreviations into your book and then write the full meaning by the side.

Av.	Gro.	Cch Opr.
Clo.	Sq.	Elec Cont.
Cres.	St.	Bldr.
Dr.	Ter.	Mkt Gdnr.
Gdns.	Wy.	Ho Furns.

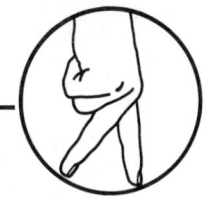

To get the best from your telephone know the number you wish to ring – check it in the directory if you are unsure. Make a note of the dialling code if you need one.

When you answer a call, which you should do promptly, give your name or the telephone number.

It is a good idea to keep a note pad near the telephone for messages. If you take a message, read it back to the caller to check that you have written it down correctly.

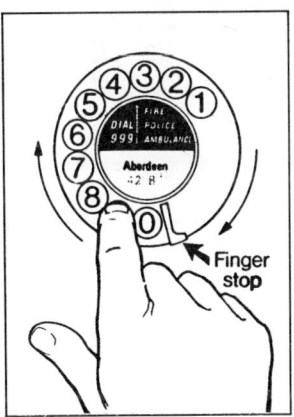

Before you start to dial a number lift the receiver, if you hear the dialling tone you may begin.

To ring **63721** place your finger on the number **6** and turn the dial firmly to the stop and let it return by itself. Do the same for **3**, **7**, **2** and **1**. Do not pause between numbers.

If you have a modern push button telephone, push the numbered buttons in the correct sequence.

Emergency Services

If you need Fire, Police, Ambulance, Coastguard, Lifeboat or Rescue Services dial **999**. When the operator answers say which service you want. Give your telephone number. When you are connected to the service, give the address or the full name of the place where help is needed. Answer any questions calmly and say what has happened.

In smoke or in the dark you may not be able to see the telephone dial. This is how to dial **999**.

1 Place a finger in each of the two holes next to the finger stop.
2 Take out the finger nearest to the stop.

3 With the remaining finger in the **9** hole, turn the dial clockwise until it reaches the finger stop.
4 Remove your finger and allow the dial to return.
5 Repeat stages **1** to **4** twice and you will have dialled **999**.

If you are using a push button telephone this is how to dial **999**.

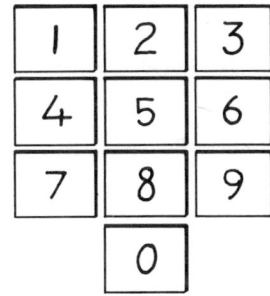

1 Lift the handset and listen for the dialling tone.
2 Feel for the buttons with your finger tips. They are in rows of three, as the picture shows.
3 The **9** button is in the right-hand bottom corner of the square formed by buttons **1** to **9**.
4 If the dialling tone stops before you start to dial, press the follow-on button, then begin to dial.
5 Press the **9** button three times, then you will have dialled **999**.

When the operator answers, ask for the service you need. Speak clearly and calmly.

Exercise 23

Work with a partner.
One of you should be the telephone caller, the other can be the receiver of the call, (later you can swop roles and repeat the exercise).

The caller should write down a message – do not let the receiver see it.
In the roles of caller and receiver give the message. The receiver should make a note of what is said.

Check the receiver's notes against the caller's original message.

PHONE ELECTRIC

Businesses often have large display entries in a telephone directory to attract attention, or like the Electricity Board, to make their numbers easier to find.

Carefully read these Electricity Board entries.

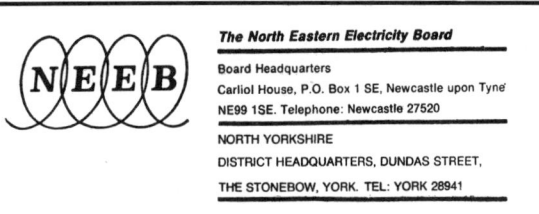

The North Eastern Electricity Board

Board Headquarters
Carliol House, P.O. Box 1 SE, Newcastle upon Tyne
NE99 1SE. Telephone: Newcastle 27520

NORTH YORKSHIRE
DISTRICT HEADQUARTERS, DUNDAS STREET,
THE STONEBOW, YORK. TEL: YORK 28941

FOR ENQUIRIES REPAIRS & FAULTS SERVICE TELEPHONE:-

District Headquarters:
Dundas Street, The Stonebow, York YO1 2PQ
(Office hours) York 28941.
(After office hours) York 28941.

Harrogate Depot: Hookstone Park, Harrogate.
(Office hours) Harrogate 885241.
(After office hours) Harrogate 885247.

Northallerton Depot: Tannery Lane, Northallerton.
(Office hours) Northallerton 2391.
(After office hours) Northallerton 2393.

Scarborough Depot: Salisbury Street.
Seamer Road, Scarborough.
(Office hours) Scarborough 74491.
(After office hours) Scarborough 74495.

Malton Depot: Norton Road, Malton.
(Office hours) Malton 2142.
(After office hours) York 28941.

Whitby Depot: Church Street, Whitby.
(Office hours) Scarborough 74491.
(After office hours) Scarborough 74495

Exercise 24

In your book, write down the following telephone numbers:

a) NEEB Board Headquarters
b) York District Headquarters
c) Northallerton (Office Hours)
d) Malton (After Office Hours)

Exercise 25

a) Which number would you ring for daytime repairs in Whitby?
b) What is the number of the after hours faults service in Scarborough?
c) Which depot has the number 885247?
d) Which area has the same number for both day and night repair services?

Affleck D, 24 Sandy Rse	**Selby** 5563
Afflick D.R, 8 Avenue Cotts,Alne	**Tollerton** 529
Afford P.J, 6 Field Close Rd,Scalby	**Scarboro** 70127
Afshar Haleh, 45 Main St,Heslington	**York** 22380
Agabeg L.S, 11 The Avenue,Haxby	**York** 769124
Agar A, 28 King Edwards Dv	**Harrogate** 55750
Agar A.R, 18 Hall Clo,Nafferton	**Driffield** 84406
Agar A.R, 30 Manorfield Rd	**Driffield** 42013
Agar Bros, Frmrs—	
Pheasant Rse, Wigginton Rd,Wigginton	**York** 768256
Villa Fm,Wigginton	**York** 769163
Agar C, 18 Chestnut Gro,Acomb	**York** 792492
Agar C, 13 Churchill Av,Burstwick	**Keyingham** 3617
Agar C, 21 Valley Rd,Darley	**Harrogate** 780295
Agar D, 1 Cherry St	**York** 51719
Agar E, 1 Brook Lodge Gdns, Norton	**Malton** 3942
Agar E, 9 The Ridings Langton Rd,Norton	**Malton** 3816
Agar Frank, 30 Knapton La,Acomb	**York** 798684
Agar G, 18 Asquith Av	**York** 33629
Agar G,Joinr,Pntr,Dectr,	
8 Sycamore Ter,Harome	**Helmsley** 578
Agar G.V, 28 High St,Burniston	**Scarboro** 870778
Agar H,Frmr, N Ghyll Fm,Farndale	**Kirkbymrside** 31644
Agar H, 4 Granville Terr,New Ellerby	**Skirlaugh** 62231
Agar H, Croft Garth,Station Rd,Ottringham	**Keyingham** 2588
Agar H.A.E, 20 Tentergate Gdns,Knaresboro	**Harrogate** 864266
Agar J,Frmr, Daneswood Fm,Danesdyke	**Bridlington** 850364
Agar J, 32 Courtneys	**Wheldrake** 450
Agar John,NFU,Mutual Avon, 12 Pinetree Av	**Rillington** 566
Agar J, Scambridge,The Mile	**Pocklington** 3114
Agar J, 10 Thoresby Av,Bempton La	**Bridlington** 76130
Agar Mrs J.A, 56 Glenroy Ter,Belle Vue St	**Scarboro** 63870
Agar J.A, 4 Pennisthorpe,Weeton	**Spurn Point** 371
Agar J.E, 291 Overdale,Southwold	**Scarboro** 583200
Agar J.E, 11 Westwood	**Scarboro** 66191
Agar J.F.H, Btchr, High St,Flamboro	**Bridlington** 850389
Agar K,Frmr, Long Acres,Firthlands Rd	**Pickering** 72164
Agar L, 30a Fortyfoot	**Bridlington** 73964
Agar Peter J, 17 Beagle Ridge Dv,Acomb	**York** 793464
Agar P.W, 3 Wold Rd,Nafferton	**Driffield** 84491
Agar R.D,Frmr, Holmefield Fm,Burton Fleming	**Thwing** 615
Agar Robert J, 126 Fulford Village	**York** 33206
Agar R.K,Pntr,Dectr, 2 Nursery Gdns,Osbaldwick	**York** 58944

Exercise 26

a) Which Helmsley number would you ring for a painter and decorator?
b) What is the number of C. Agar, 18 Chestnut Grove?
c) Which number would you ring for J. Agar, of The Mile?
d) Who lives at Harrogate 780295?
e) Who lives at York 793464?
f) Which number would you ring for a butcher in Bridlington?
g) Give the telephone number of a joiner.
h) How many farmers are listed?
i) If you wanted someone to do some woodwork, painting and decorating, who would you ring, and what would the number be?
j) Who is the NFU representative?

In an ordinary telephone directory subscribers are listed alphabetically. Mr Jones the electrician is listed under **J** for **Jones**. You would not be able to find his number under **E** for **electrician**.

® *Registered trademark of British Telecommunications plc in the U.K.*

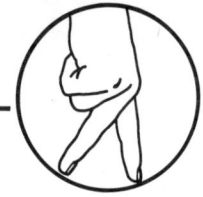

In a Yellow Pages Directory you would find many electricians listed under **E**.

This is because the Yellow Pages is a directory of businesses and telephone numbers. Each telephone area has its own Yellow Pages volume. Its aim is to make it easier for customers to find the goods and services they need.

There are two ways to find what you want. If it is something simple like a hospital, look under **H** for **hospital**. If you do not know how the service you want is listed, you must turn to the index at the back of the directory. If you cannot find what you want, try looking for something similar.

Example
If you are unable to find a cabinet-maker, try looking for someone else who works with wood. Try looking under 'Woodworkers' where you will find cabinet-makers, carpenters and joiners.

Exercise 27

Read the index below and then write down your answers.

a) Under which other heading could you look for word processing equipment?
b) Where else could you find woodworker's supplies?
c) Where would you look for someone to control woodworm?
d) Under which headings would you find word processing services?

Exercise 28

Make up an entry of your own to go in this **W** index.

Woodworkers
—See also Cabinet makers Carpenters & joiners
Woodworkers' supplies
—See also Cabinet makers' supplies
Woodworking machinery
Woodworm, dry rot & damp control
—See also Pest & vermin control services
Waterproofing services Wood preservation services
Wool & hair brokers
Wool shops
Woollen goods mfrs & merchants
Woollen & worsted cloth mfrs
—See also Worsteds—Fine fancy Mfrs
Woollen & worsted merchants
Word processing eqpt—See Computer systems & eqpt
Word processing services
—See also Secretarial & office services
Work bench mfrs.

Exercise 29

Read the computer systems equipment advertisements/entries on page 17, then answer these questions:

a) Why have some firms paid to have large displays?
b) Who offers an electronic service?
c) Which telephone number would you ring to get a word processor in Bradford?
d) Who offers a data processing service in Hull?
e) Where will you be able to buy a computer in York?
f) What is the STD dialling code for Leeds?
g) What is the STD dialling code for Hull?
h) Whose telephone number is 0532-458726?
i) What services are available at Bridlington 77115?

Exercise 30

Design an eye-catching entry for your own computer company or service.

Exercise 31

Arrange this list of services in the order you would find them in a telephone directory. Write them down, using your local Yellow Pages to find a telephone number for each of them.

Chemist	Sports Shop	Launderette
Doctor	Bookseller	Video Shop
Hairdressser	Abattoir	Garage
Airline	Library	Bank

Exercise 32

Make notes ready for a telephone call to your local repair and faults service. Your electric water heater has stopped working and you need it mended quickly.

Exercise 33

Look in your local directory for these numbers:

a) your school
b) your doctor
c) the nearest hospital
d) the local police station

Exercise 34

Arrange these entries in the order you would find them in a telephone directory:

A.C.T. Ltd., Agric Mrcnts, A.P.P. Builders, A.C. Cars, A.B.C. Taxis, A.L. Fuels, A.B.C. Cinema, A.L. Coal Supplies, A.R.C. Concrete, A.H. Haulage, A.B.V. Plumbing, A.T.C. Engineers, A.I. Service,

Wordsearch

Look for these words in the *wordsearch* below:

Subscriber	Builder
Customers	Directory
Message	Order
Newsagent	Dialling Tone
Enquiries	Surname
Lists	Operator
Index	Address
Connected	Yellow Pages
Photographer	Alphabetical
Headquarters	Dialling Code
Occupation	Exchange
Faults	Farmer
Repairs	Initials
Receiver	Telephone
Abbreviated	Emergency Services

```
W A K L C F A U L T S T A H O B K Q I
X X E G N A H C X E N Q U I R I E S G
M E J I U R B U K M E S S A G E M U V
R Y D C Q M L S S E R D D A E U J R Q
E E S N A E A T C R H G R L N S H N M
C L D C I R C O F G R E D R O R D A G
E L I L N F I M L E T R N E T E V M H
I O R E I L T E J N N J O H G T V E O
V W E N T U E R Q C E L I P N R D R K
E P C O I B B S F Y G P T A I A E L H
R A T H A N A E S S A O A R L U T X O
E G O P L M H S T E S N P G L Q A P S
P E R E S G P M S R W V U O A D I W G
A S Y L K U L F I V E K C T I A V M N
I X C E D I A L L I N G C O D E E L C
R D E T C E N N O C B O O H J H R X G
S C T V R O T A R E P O B P I B B E T
N X X K E C N P S S U B S C R I B E R
K J D S A U U N C B M V W J X P A T E
```

5 Money matters

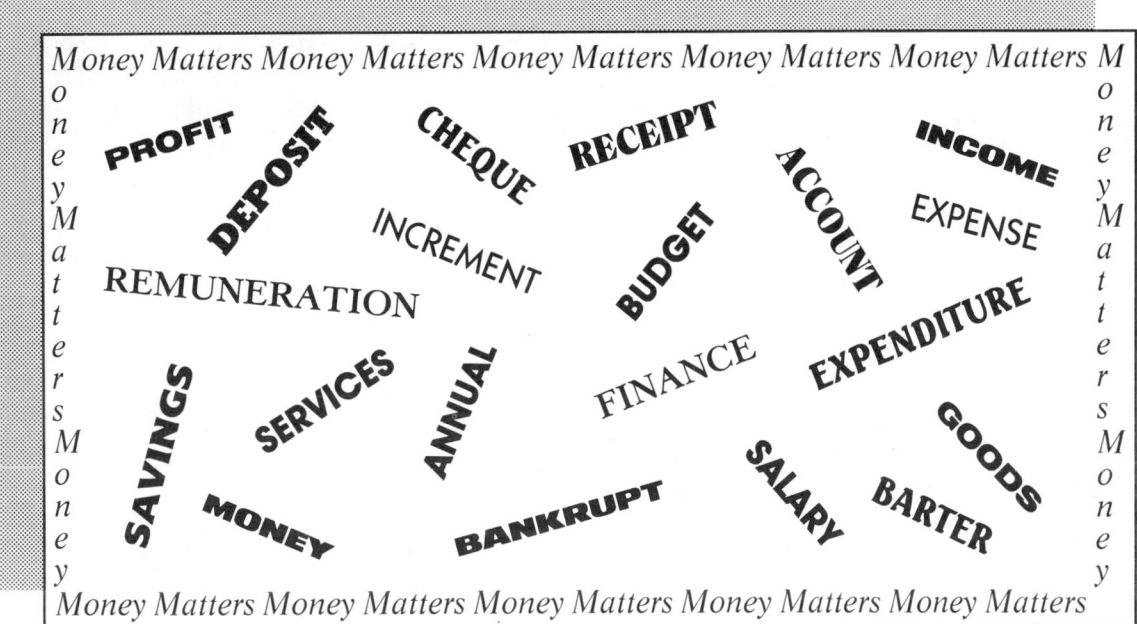

Money Matters Money Matters Money Matters Money Matters Money Matters

PROFIT DEPOSIT CHEQUE RECEIPT INCOME EXPENSE INCREMENT REMUNERATION BUDGET ACCOUNT SAVINGS SERVICES ANNUAL FINANCE EXPENDITURE GOODS MONEY BANKRUPT SALARY BARTER

Money Matters Money Matters Money Matters Money Matters Money Matters

All of the words above have something to do with money. Do you know what they mean? Do you understand enough to balance a budget? Or write out a cheque?

The examples and exercises in this unit will help you to understand budgeting, payslips, bank accounts and services, income tax, insurance and building societies.

Exercise 35

Sort out the words at the top of this page. Put them in alphabetical order and write down the meaning of those you know. Use a dictionary to check any uncertainties.

Exercise 36

Write your answers to these questions in sentences.
Remember – a sentence begins with a capital letter and ends with a full stop.

a) Do you have to pay for anything weekly?
b) Do you buy comics, magazines or books?
c) Do you pay for your own clothes?
d) Are you given pocket money?
e) Do you have a part-time job?
f) Do you save any money?

Example
Jane has a part-time job and receives pocket money from her parents. Her weekly income is fifteen pounds. She has to buy her own clothes and pay for other things. Here is her weekly budget:

	£ p
Magazines	0.50
Make-up	1.10
Clothes	3.40
Bus Fares	2.00
Spending money	4.00
Savings	4.00
Total	15.00

Exercise 37

Make a similar budget for your average weekly spending.

Exercise 38

When you have left school, you may go to college or have a job. If you still live at home, what else will you have to add to your budget?

Example

Tom earns £75 a week as a butcher. Here is his budget:

	£ p
Board/keep	17.50
Transport	7.50
Clothes	10.00
Spending	15.00
Savings	25.00
Total	75.00

Exercise 39

If Tom lived away from home, what other items would he have to include in his budget?
Talk about them with a partner.

Example

Alison lives in a small flat which costs her £25 per week. She earns £80 a week working in an office. Here is her budget:

	£ p
Rent	25.00
Food	15.00
Clothes	10.00
Spending	10.00
Bus fares	5.00
Savings	15.00
Total	80.00

Exercise 40

Work out a weekly budget for each of these young people.

a) Robert is an apprentice joiner. He earns £90.50 a week. He shares a flat with two other people, the rent is £48.00 a week. He spends £15.00 a week on food and puts £10.00 towards bills. He saves £20.00.

b) Susan is a nanny. She lives with the family she works for and has no living expenses. She earns £40.50 a week. She saves £10.00, she spends £12.50 on her clothes and make-up, the rest she spends on bus fares and going out.

Exercise 41

In a small group talk about these methods of saving. Work out the advantages and disadvantages of each way of saving:

Piggybank/Post Office/Building Society/Bank

Exercise 42

Write out a list of things you will have to pay for when you have left school. Compare your list with a partner. Are there any differences? Decide which are the five most important things.

When you leave school you will have a regular income of some sort. This may be unemployment benefit, a grant or a wage. You will need to be able to manage your own money.

If you go into a job when you leave school, your employer will pay you a wage. You may be paid either weekly or monthly.

Exercise 43

With a partner talk about weekly and monthly pay. Work out the advantages and disadvantages of each. One of you can adopt the role of the worker and the other can play the employer. Discuss the methods of paying workers and say which is preferable.

When you are paid your employer will give you a pay slip. This is a notice which you get in your pay packet. It shows you how much you have earned and the deductions which have been made. You should keep your pay slips in a safe place, in case you need them. You may have to show them to tax or social security officers.

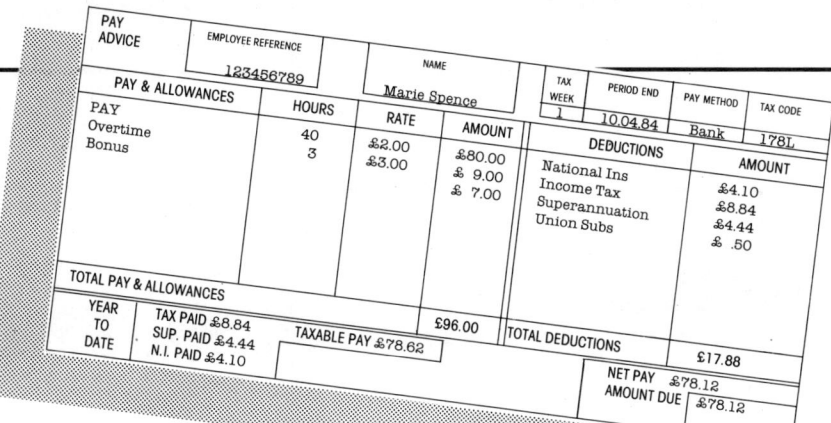

PAY ADVICE	EMPLOYEE REFERENCE 123456789		NAME Marie Spence		TAX WEEK 1	PERIOD END 10.04.84	PAY METHOD Bank	TAX CODE 178L

PAY & ALLOWANCES	HOURS	RATE	AMOUNT		
PAY			£80.00		
Overtime	40	£2.00	£ 9.00	DEDUCTIONS	AMOUNT
Bonus	3	£3.00	£ 7.00	National Ins	£4.10
				Income Tax	£8.84
				Superannuation	£4.44
				Union Subs	£ .50

TOTAL PAY & ALLOWANCES				
YEAR TO DATE	TAX PAID £8.84 SUP. PAID £4.44 N.I. PAID £4.10	TAXABLE PAY £78.62	£96.00	TOTAL DEDUCTIONS £17.88
				NET PAY £78.12
				AMOUNT DUE £78.12

This is Marie Spence's pay slip.

Exercise 44

Here are some words from Marie's pay slip. You will find them on most other pay slips. Read them carefully, look up each word in a dictionary and then match each word with one of the meanings below.

Words	Meanings
Employee	Money earned before deductions
Pay	Take home pay
Overtime	A person employed
Bonus	Pay liable to tax
National Insurance	Money for working extra hours
Income tax	Money earned
Superannuation	Money paid for efficiency
Union Subscription	Money paid to the Government
Deductions	Fee paid to a trade union
Net pay	Money paid for a pension
Taxable pay	Money paid to the Government to pay for social security

Example
Marie's basic wage is the amount she earns for her 40-hour working week. That is £80.00.

Exercise 45

Read Marie's pay slip carefully, then write out your answers to these questions:

a) How many hours of overtime has Marie worked?

b) What is Marie's gross wage?
c) How much was deducted from Marie's pay?
d) How was Marie paid?
e) How much does Marie earn per hour?
f) How much tax has Marie paid?
g) How much will Marie pay to her union each year?

There are three ways in which an employer can pay wages:

cash
cheque
directly into a bank account

Exercise 46

a) Write down the advantages and disadvantages of each way of paying wages.
b) Which two methods of paying wages mean that Marie would need a bank account?

Exercise 47

Make out a pay slip for yourself. Include as many sections in your pay slip as you need.

Exercise 48

Make out the following pay slip:

Employee: Peter Smith.

Employee reference no: 789654.

Tax week 3. Tax code 178L.

Pay	£100.00
Overtime	37.50
National ins	5.60
Income tax	33.00
Union subs	.60
Net pay	???.??
Amount due	???.??

Income tax & school leavers

This leaflet is to help you to understand something about the income tax system and how it will affect you after you leave school.

IR 33

What happens to the money I pay?

You pay income tax to help towards the cost of services we all receive in this country. A few examples are the National Health Service, Defence, and Social Security benefits. The Chancellor of the Exchequer announces his Budget at the beginning of each tax year. He says how much money he needs and how it is going to be spent. Some of his proposals will affect the tax you pay.

What do I pay tax on?

You will normally pay tax on all kinds of earnings including tips, bonuses and part-time work. If you have invested any savings you will also pay tax on most interest you receive. Some Savings Bank interest is tax-free, and tax on any interest from a Building Society is paid by the Society before you receive it. Some Social Security benefits are taxed but others are not. For example, unemployment benefit is taxable, but not child benefit.

Does this mean I pay tax on everything I earn?

Everyone can earn or receive a certain amount of income without paying tax. This is called the single person's allowance and you are allowed the full amount even if you only work for part of the tax year. A married man can claim a larger allowance, and if his wife works an allowance is given against her earnings. There are also extra allowances for single parents, the blind and people who support a dependent relative. The total of your personal allowances is the amount you can earn in the tax year without paying tax. It is your tax-free pay.

Can I claim expenses?

The cost of tools or special clothing which you need at work can sometimes be claimed if they are not provided by your employer. But you cannot claim for National Insurance Contributions or for the cost of travelling to and from work.

All people who earn over a certain amount of money in the tax year will pay income tax; if you are employed, you will pay tax under a system known as PAYE, *pay as you earn*. Each time you are paid, an amount of money is taken from your wages and paid to the Inland Revenue – this is income tax.

The tax year does not follow the calendar from January to December. It begins on 6th April one year and ends on 5th April the next year.

Before you leave school you will probably be given a leaflet called *Income tax and school leavers*. This leaflet answers many of the questions which people always ask about tax.

Exercise 49

a) For which services does income tax pay?
b) Who decides how much money is needed to pay for these services?
c) Apart from wages, what else is taxed?
d) Is child benefit taxable?
e) What is a single person's allowance?
f) What is the total of your personal allowances?
g) What expenses can you claim?

Exercise 50

Imagine that you are 18 and work in a factory. Which of the following could you claim as expenses?

a) bus fares
b) petrol money for your motor bike
c) the cost of shoes with a steel toecap to protect your feet
d) your trade union subscriptions
e) the cost of buying your own tools for your job as factory electrician

Exercise 51

Work with a partner. One of you should play the part of a tax officer, the other a worker. The tax officer should explain which earnings will be taxed.

When do I start to pay income tax?

You will probably start to pay tax when you get your first job.

If you go straight to a job when you leave school, your employer will give you a simple form. You can sign it to say that this is your first regular job since leaving school. He will send the form to the tax office to tell them that you have started work.

Your employer will also give you a coding claim form. This may seem more difficult because it has to be used by other people, some of them with more complicated tax affairs than yours. If you have other income as well as the earnings from your new job, use this form to tell the tax office. Also use it if you want to claim extra allowances. Your employer will give you an addressed envelope if you want to send the form yourself. But if you do not mind him seeing your completed claim he will send it for you. If you do not need to use the coding claim form, keep it because it gives information which you may find useful later.

If you have claimed unemployment benefit before starting work, your employer will have to treat you as though you were coming from another job.

Exercise 52

Copy this paragraph and fill in the spaces with suitable words.

Most people begin to pay --- when they start their first ---. A person who goes straight from ------ to a job, will be given a ---- to fill in. The employer will send this to the --- ------ to tell them that this person has started ----. Then an -------- will give a -------- a coding ----- ----. If you earn ----- elsewhere you can use this form to tell the --- ------. You can also use this form if you need to claim extra ----------. Your employer will give you a special addressed -------- so that you can ---- the form yourself.

How is my tax worked out?

If you have not claimed unemployment benefit, your first employer will give you a PAYE code. This code will be based on the single person's allowance. If you use the coding claim form, your PAYE code may have to be changed. The tax office will work out what extra allowances or income to take into account. They will send you a new code and show you how it was worked out. They will also send your new code to your employer who will use it to tax your pay.

Your PAYE code represents your tax-free pay for the year. Your employer will use this code with 'tax tables' which spread your tax-free pay between the number of pay days in the tax year, 52 if you are paid weekly or 12 if you are paid monthly. On each pay day the tables show the right amount of tax-free pay to be subtracted from your earnings and you only pay tax on what is left.

If for any reason you are not paid for a while, the tax-free pay for those weeks builds up until it can be subtracted from your earnings on a later pay day. If your earnings are less than your tax-free pay at any time then of course you do not pay any tax.

If you claimed unemployment benefit before starting work, you will get a form P45 from your benefit office to give to your employer. More is said about this form below. It will tell your employer what code he must use for you. Until he gets it, he will have to use a special 'emergency code'.

What is this PAYE?

PAYE stands for Pay As You Earn. This means just what it says, you pay your tax as you go along. Each time you are paid, the right amount of tax will be taken from your pay, as long as you have the right PAYE code.

What happens if I change my job?

It is very important to get a form P45 from your employer when you leave a job. This is a leaving certificate which shows your PAYE code, your total earnings and how much tax you have paid since the start of the tax year.

Your PAYE code is a number followed by a letter. This shows how much you can earn before paying tax. This number is your allowances without the last figure. £3295 = 329.

The code number is usually followed by the letter **L** or **H**.

H means a married man.

L means a single person or a working wife.

Every year your tax office will send you a notice of coding and a leaflet, the Coding Guide, to help you to understand it.

Example

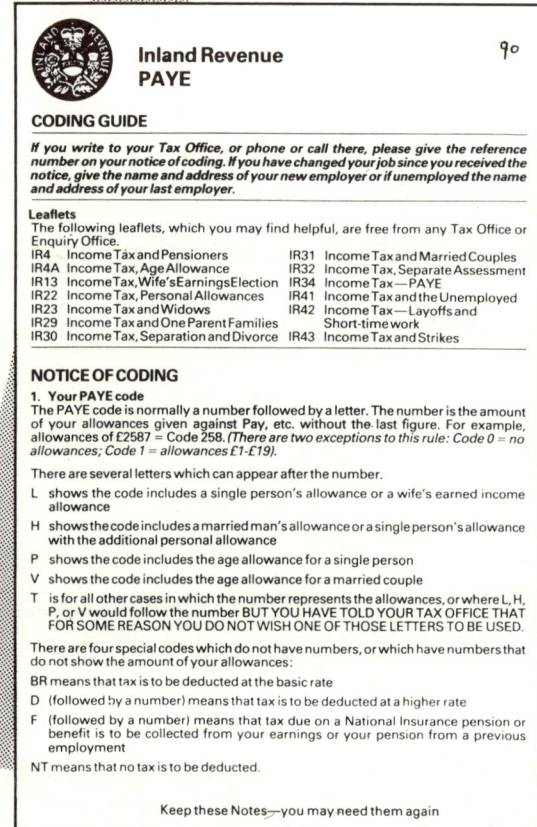

CODING GUIDE

If you write to your Tax Office, or phone or call there, please give the reference number on your notice of coding. If you have changed your job since you received the notice, give the name and address of your new employer or if unemployed the name and address of your last employer.

Leaflets
The following leaflets, which you may find helpful, are free from any Tax Office or Enquiry Office.
IR4 Income Tax and Pensioners   IR31 Income Tax and Married Couples
IR4A Income Tax, Age Allowance   IR32 Income Tax, Separate Assessment
IR13 Income Tax, Wife's Earnings Election IR34 Income Tax—PAYE
IR22 Income Tax, Personal Allowances   IR41 Income Tax and the Unemployed
IR23 Income Tax and Widows   IR42 Income Tax—Layoffs and
IR29 Income Tax and One Parent Families   Short-time work
IR30 Income Tax, Separation and Divorce   IR43 Income Tax and Strikes

NOTICE OF CODING

1. Your PAYE code
The PAYE code is normally a number followed by a letter. The number is the amount of your allowances given against Pay, etc. without the last figure. For example, allowances of £2587 = Code 258. *(There are two exceptions to this rule: Code 0 = no allowances; Code 1 = allowances £1-£19).*

There are several letters which can appear after the number.

L   shows the code includes a single person's allowance or a wife's earned income allowance

H   shows the code includes a married man's allowance or a single person's allowance with the additional personal allowance

P   shows the code includes the age allowance for a single person

V   shows the code includes the age allowance for a married couple

T   is for all other cases in which the number represents the allowances, or where L, H, P, or V would follow the number BUT YOU HAVE TOLD YOUR TAX OFFICE THAT FOR SOME REASON YOU DO NOT WISH ONE OF THOSE LETTERS TO BE USED.

There are four special codes which do not have numbers, or which have numbers that do not show the amount of your allowances:

BR means that tax is to be deducted at the basic rate

D   (followed by a number) means that tax is to be deducted at a higher rate

F   (followed by a number) means that tax due on a National Insurance pension or benefit is to be collected from your earnings or your pension from a previous employment

NT means that no tax is to be deducted.

Keep these Notes—you may need them again

Exercise 53

Read the Coding Guide. When you have read it, write out this paragraph and fill in the missing words.

If you have a problem and need to write, visit or t-------- your --- Office, you should give the --------- number on your ------ of coding. If you have changed your --- since you received the ------, you should give the ---- and ------- of your new -------- or if you are u--------- the name and address of your ---- employer.

Exercise 54

Write down the answers to these questions:

a) Can you tell whether a woman is married by reading her PAYE code? Give a reason.

b) What does the PAYE code 244H tell you about the person who is paying tax?

c) If your allowances were not correct on your notice of coding, what would you do about it?

d) What is the address and telephone number of your local tax office? (Try the telephone directory.)

Exercise 55

Copy and complete the following:

a) Basic wage is the money you get in a normal working week without including …

b) The money you take home is called your…

c) Overtime is any extra time worked after normal …

d) Deductions are …

e) The Inland Revenue collects …

Exercise 56

With a partner complete these tasks:

a) Telephone your Local Tax Office and ask for the leaflet which tells you about Income Tax and the Unemployed.

b) Imagine that you work in the Citizens Advice Bureau. A visitor asks for information about Income Tax and Personal Allowances. Explain which leaflet he or she should ask for.

Exercise 57

Write a letter to your Inspector of Taxes. In it point out that your notice of coding does not appear to include the flat rate deduction for replacing and maintaining tools. This has been agreed between your trade union and the Inland Revenue.

Remember the correct layout for a formal letter.
Look back at page 5.

Social Security

Many countries have some sort of social security system, which makes sure that people get help when they need it. In Britain our social security system is paid for by national insurance (NI) contributions, and taxes. All working people pay NI contributions.

The sorts of help people get in return for paying contributions and taxes are known as 'benefits'.

The five main benefits are:

1 for people who can't find work
2 for the person bringing up a child
3 for people who are on a low income
4 for families on a low wage
5 for people who have retired

Benefits **1** and **5** are contributory. This means that a person must have paid the appropriate NI contributions to benefit.
Benefit **2** is noncontributory.

Exercise 58

Match each of the benefits **A** to **E** below to one of the definitions **1** to **5** above. Write your answers in complete sentences.
e.g. Unemployment benefit is + *definition*.

A Child benefit
B Retirement benefit
C Unemployment benefit
D Supplementary benefit
E Family income supplement

Shortly before you leave school you will be sent a card showing you your NI number. Keep this card in a safe place. When you are working your employer will need to know your number.

If you are ill and are unable to work for at least four days in a row you may receive SSP, that is *Statutory Sick Pay*. This will be paid by your employer.

When you begin to work your employer should tell you what to do in case of illness. He should tell you how to let him know that you are not fit for work.

Exercise 59

Imagine that you are ill. You decide you cannot go to work.

a) You telephone your employer to say that you are ill and will not be at work.
b) You are no better the next day, so you go to see your doctor. He or she gives you a medical certificate.

Write a letter to your employer to say what is the matter with you.

"Sickness benefit – you cannot get sickness benefit for as long as you receive Statutory Sick Pay (SSP) from your employer. If your employer will not give you SSP or you are still sick when your sick pay finishes or you are self-employed, unemployed or non-employed you can get sickness benefit if you've paid a set amount of contributions or if you can't work as the result of an industrial accident or prescribed disease."
NP.12/April 83

Exercise 60

When you have read the extract from pamphlet NP.12/April 83, answer all of the following questions:

a) When can you not receive SSP?
b) If you are unemployed, when can you get sickness benefit?
c) What type of accident would entitle you to sickness benefit?

If you want some help or advice, if you do not understand something to do with benefits, ask at once. If you have a question about social security benefits contact your local Social Security office – its address will be in the telephone directory.

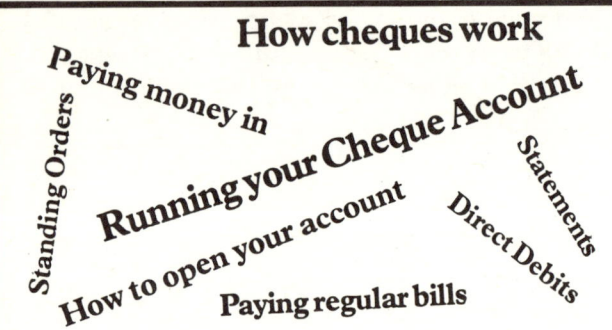

How cheques work

Paying money in

Standing Orders

Running your Cheque Account

How to open your account

Statements

Direct Debits

Paying regular bills

If you have never had a bank account you might ask: who needs a bank account? The answer is simple: *you* do.

When you are leaving school, starting a job, joining a scheme, going to college, a bank account can help you to manage your money.

Your employer may pay wages straight into a bank, so you will need to open an account for that. You may be paid by cheque and a bank account will help to turn a cheque into cash. Even if you are paid in cash, a bank account may be a safe place to keep your money.

Whichever way you are paid, the big banks have services to help you to make the most of your money.

Here are three advantages of a bank account:

1 your money is safe and well looked after
2 you can withdraw cash when you need it
3 you can pay bills by cheque or pay for goods in shops

The two most popular types of bank account are current accounts or deposit accounts.

With a current account:

    you may use cheques
    withdraw cash
    pay in cheques or cash
    the bank charges you for services

With a deposit account:

    the bank pays you interest
    you can more easily save money

Give a Young Person a Good Start

There are four main banks in England. They are known as the big four clearing banks. *Clearing* simply means that they allow customers to draw cheques on their current accounts and then the banks who receive the cheques send them through the clearing system to the appropriate branch.

All of the banks are very keen to attract young customers. They have made opening an account very easy.

NatWest

Exercise 61

Which bank is missing from the list of the big four shown above? If you do not know, look around as you pass through your town. Find the missing bank and draw its sign.

When you decide to open a bank account, just choose a bank, step inside and talk to the staff. Go to the enquiries desk where you will be asked to fill in a form.

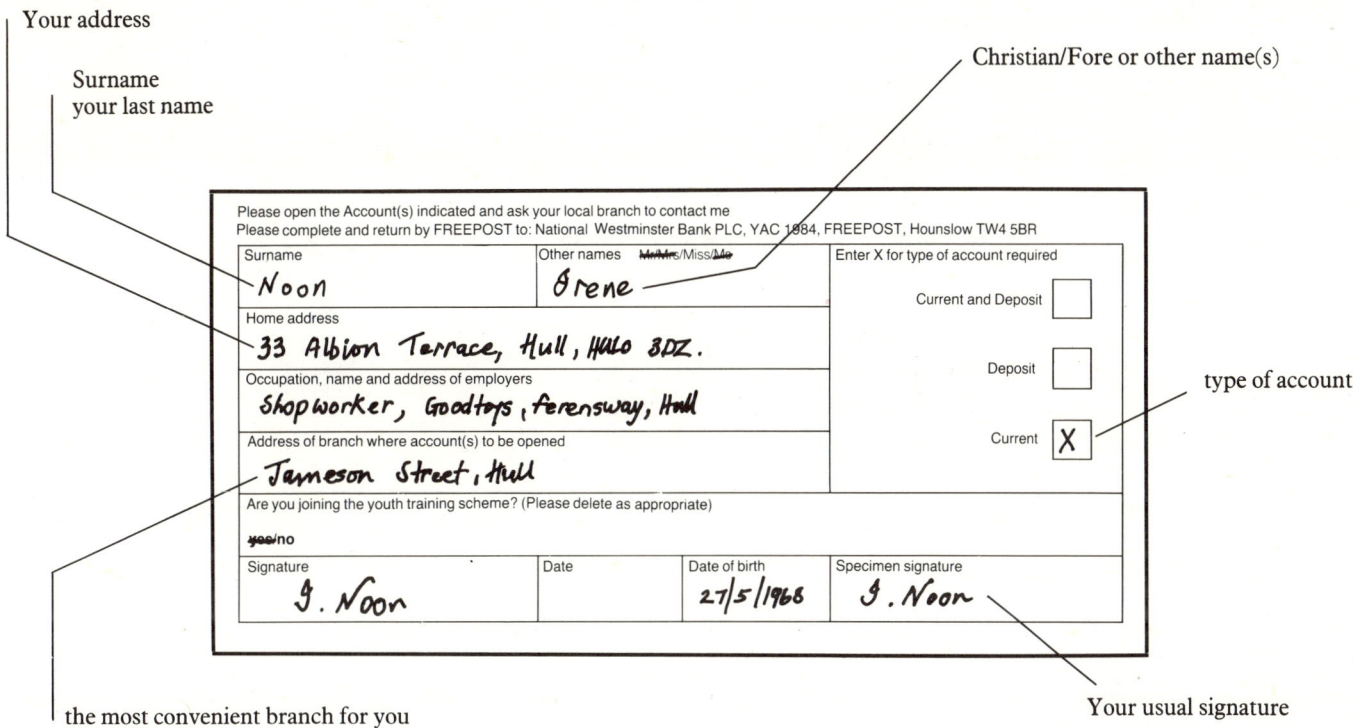

Your address

Surname
your last name

Christian/Fore or other name(s)

Please open the Account(s) indicated and ask your local branch to contact me
Please complete and return by FREEPOST to: National Westminster Bank PLC, YAC 1884, FREEPOST, Hounslow TW4 5BR

Surname	Other names ~~Mr/Mrs~~/Miss/~~Ms~~	Enter X for type of account required
Noon	Irene	

Home address
33 Albion Terrace, Hull, HU10 3DZ.

Occupation, name and address of employers
Shopworker, Goodtoys, Ferensway, Hull

Address of branch where account(s) to be opened
Jameson Street, Hull

Current and Deposit ☐

Deposit ☐

Current ☒

type of account

Are you joining the youth training scheme? (Please delete as appropriate)
~~yes~~/no

Signature	Date	Date of birth	Specimen signature
I. Noon		27/5/1968	I. Noon

the most convenient branch for you

Your usual signature

Exercise 62

Draw an application form like the one above. Fill it in using your personal details.

If you want a bank account through which you can do your day-to-day business, you will need a current account. This is a good, safe place to put your money if you need to use it at short notice.

The bank will also offer you several useful services to help you to manage your money. If you want to keep your money in a safe place and earn interest you can open a deposit account. With ths type of account, you deposit your money in the bank, the bank will use the money to earn interest for you until you want to use some of it.

If you open a current account most banks will offer the following services:

   a cheque book
   regular bank statements
   standing orders and direct debits
   automated teller machine card
   cheque card

How your account works for you

Your cheque book will allow you to draw money from the bank. You will be able to buy things without having to carry a lot of money and you will be able to pay bills quickly and safely.

A cheque is a written order to your bank, telling it to pay somebody with some of the money in your account. You can give a shopkeeper a cheque (supported by a cheque card), and you can send them through the post.

When you use cheques you always have a record of the payments which you have made.

Exercise 63

Work with a partner.
One of you should take the part of the bank manager and the other the new customer.

Work out a short role-play sequence in which the customer is interviewed by the bank manager. Explain the advantages of cheques.

Writing cheques

Pay
The name of the person you want to pay

Date

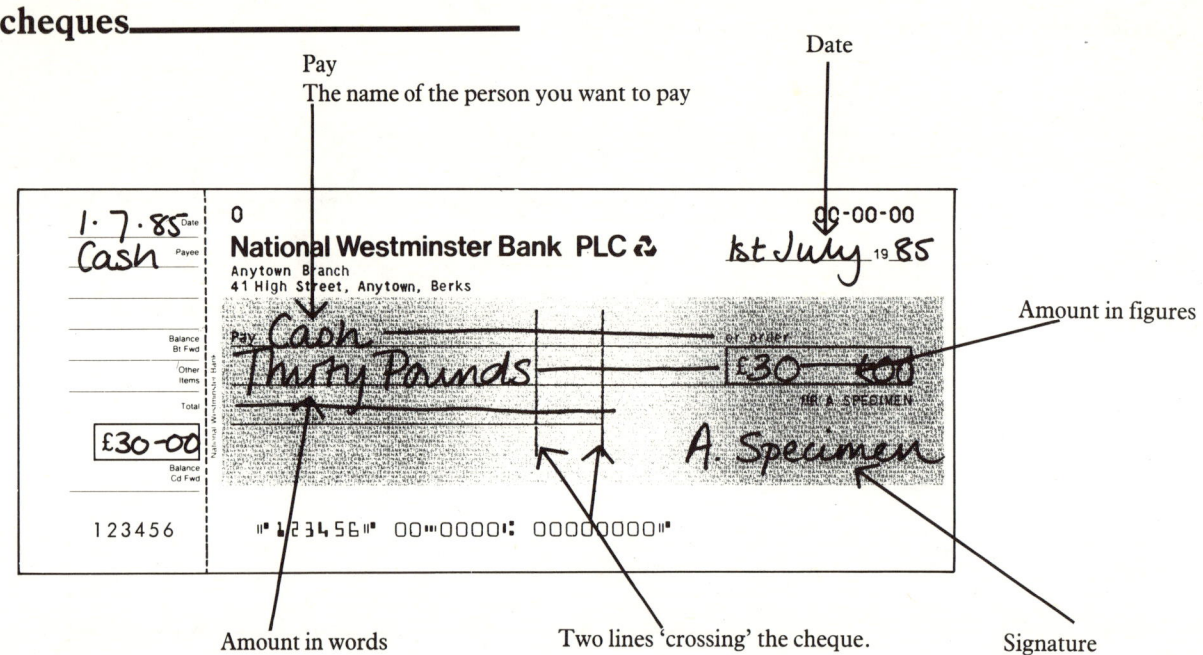

Amount in figures

Amount in words

Two lines 'crossing' the cheque.

Signature

Making out a cheque is easy because the banks have designed simple, safe cheque forms like the one shown at the top of this page.

To make out a cheque, simply write:

1 the name of the person you wish to pay, (the payee) or cash if you are withdrawing money
2 the amount you want to pay, in words and figures
3 the date
4 your signature
5 draw lines through any blank spaces
6 record the details on the cheque stub

Along the bottom of every cheque you can see a row of figures, in groups. These figures help the bank to run your account. From the left they are: the cheque number, the bank code number and your personal account number. Your name will also be printed on every cheque.

Exercise

Draw three cheques like the one above and make them out to:
a) the Electricity Board for £35.75p
b) cash for £45.00
c) A1 Insurance PLC for £22.15p

There are two kinds of cheque: open and crossed. A *crossed* cheque has two vertical lines drawn down the middle. This means that the payee can only pay the cheque into a bank account. It cannot be cashed by the wrong person. An *open* cheque can be cashed without going through a bank account.

If you want to withdraw cash from your bank, you write *pay cash* between the vertical lines and sign the alteration.

Your bank manager may let you have a cheque card. This enables you to draw up to £50 cash at any branch of the bank. It will also guarantee any cheques you give to other people up to £50.

Once you have opened your account, you can pay cash or cheques into it. Paying-in slips will be printed for you, with your name, branch and account number. You simply write in the amount that you are paying in and sign it.

You can pay in at any branch, or through the post. But, you should not send cash unless by registered mail.

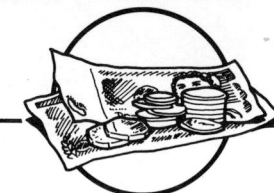

Paying-in

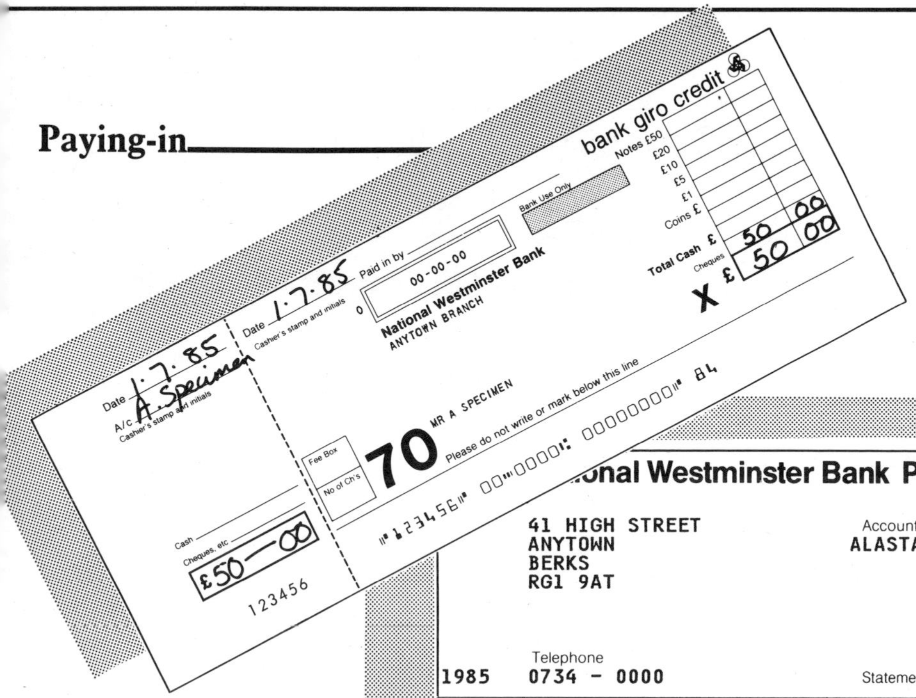
Date 1.7.85
A/c A. Specimen
Cashier's stamp and initials
Cash
Cheques, etc. £50—00
123456

Date 1.7.85
Cashier's stamp and initials
Fee Box
No of Ch's
bank giro credit
Paid in by
00-00-00
National Westminster Bank
ANYTOWN BRANCH
Bank Use Only
70 MR A SPECIMEN
Notes £50
£20
£10
£5
£1
Coins £
Total Cash £ 50 00
Cheques X £ 50 00
Please do not write or mark below this line
⑈123456⑈ 00⑈0000⑆ 00000000⑈ 84

National Westminster Bank PLC **CONFIDENTIAL**

41 HIGH STREET
ANYTOWN
BERKS
RG1 9AT

Account CURRENT
ALASTAIR SPECIMEN

SHEET NO 12

Telephone
1985 0734 - 0000

Statement date 20 FEB 1985 Account no. 20127944

Date	Details		Withdrawals	Deposits	Balance
2JAN	Balance from Sheet no. 11				2.48
7JAN	WAGES			253.00	255.48
18JAN		000018	20.00		235.48
21JAN		000017	84.50		150.98
25JAN		000020	12.62		138.36
4FEB		000019	16 84		121.52
8FEB	BOOK CLUB	DD	12.50		109.02
18FEB	ANYTOWN			2.36	111.38
20FEB	KINGS CROSS	AC	10.00		101.38

Bank Statements

These are complete records of cheques written and payments made into an account, as well as details of standing orders or direct debits which you have authorised the bank to pay from the account.

You can check the bank statement against your paying-in slips and cheque book stubs.

Your bank statement will use some special words and abbreviations, you will need to learn them.

Details	details of each transaction
Debits	money paid from the account
Credits	money paid into the account
Balance	the amount in the account
DD	direct debit
SO	standing order
AC	automated cash withdrawal

Your bank will send you a statement at regular intervals.

Exercise 65

Look carefully at John England's statement and answer these questions:

a) Where did he withdraw £10?
b) To whom did he pay £12.50p by DD?
c) Where did he withdraw £10 in cash?
d) When were his wages paid into the bank?
e) What was his balance on January 25th?
f) How did he withdraw £10?
g) For how much did he write a cheque number 000017?

Exercise 66

Draw an outline bank statement and record the following transactions:

a) Pay in £92.73p in wages
b) Withdraw £15 cash
c) Pay F.J. Anderson £7.22p with cheque number 001234
d) Credit £17.50p in cash and cheques
e) Direct debit to bookclub for £6.35p

Standing Orders and Direct Debits

Your bank provides services which save you time and inconvenience. Standing orders and direct debits are a good example. If you have regular bills such as insurance premiums, rates or subscriptions you can arrange for the bank to pay them automatically from your account at the correct time.

A **standing order** is an instruction which you give to your bank. It tells the bank to pay a certain amount of money to a named person on a specific date.

Example
Pay Road Runners Club £25 on the 1st of March annually.

A **direct debit** is a little different. You tell the bank to accept debits for your account from a named person or company, for a certain amount on a specified date.

Exercise 67

Write a letter to a bank manager, tell him to pay £37.75p to the friendly Finance Co PLC, on the 17th of every month for twenty-four months. Remember to tell the bank when to start and finish payments.

Travel cheques

Travel cheques let you take your money abroad safely. They are very safe, because they can be replaced if they are lost or stolen. Banks can issue travellers cheques in most currencies. It is a good idea to take cheques in the currency of the country you are visiting, this makes encashment easier.

Exercise 68

a) How could you tell if a cheque has been crossed?
b) How can an open cheque be misused?
c) Who is a payee?
d) What should you write on a cheque stub?
e) Can you draw cheques on a deposit account?

Exercise 69

If you lose your cheque book you should tell your bank manager straight away.

Jean Young lost her cheque book on the 29th May. It contained ten cheques, numbered from 000015 to 000025. She telphoned the bank immediately. The bank manager asked her to write a letter to confirm the information which she gave over the telephone. Jean lives at 45 Rectory Gardens, Durham City.

Write Jean's letter for her; set it out properly.

Exercise 70

Make out a bank statement for this customer. Use the information given below.

Name: Joan Marsh
Account number: 12345678

Debits		Date		Credits
£10.00	000001	1/3		
£17.50	000005	3/3		
£25.99	000008	10/3		
		26/2	Salary	£276.65
		2/3	Cash/chqs	£58.50
£15.00	S.O.	6/3		
£35.00	D.D	12/3		
£50.00	000002	13/3		
£ 7.95	000003	13/3		
£ 5.99	000006	19/3		
£11.00	000007	20/3		

Exercise 71

Choose one of these items and give a short talk about it:
a) cheque and deposit accounts
b) bank statements
c) making the most of your bank account

As well as the services already mentioned your bank will be able to provide these services:

1 foreign currency
2 administer your estate
3 buy and sell stocks and shares
4 provide a credit card
5 arrange a loan
6 arrange insurance
7 give advice on many financial matters

Insurance

If you own valuable things you can protect them against loss, damage or theft through an insurance policy.

Exercise 72

With a partner talk about the valuable things which you own now. You may have a camera, a computer or some jewellery. Make a list of the items which would cost a lot of money to replace.

Think ahead to when you have a home of your own. What extra things will need to be protected against loss, damage or theft? List them.

Before you go any further into the world of insurance you had better be sure that you understand the words used to talk about insurance.

Exercise 73

Match the insurance words in column **A** to the meanings in column **B**.

A	B
policy	* the price quoted as the cost of insurance
premium	* the document setting out a contract between an insurance company and a customer
quotation	* ask an insurance company to pay for damage etc.
cover	* the annual cost of your insurance
third party	* a reduction in cost as you have not made any claims
comprehensive	
claim	* a person who sells and advises about insurance
no claims bonus	* a person not involved in an accident or argument
broker	* risks which will be paid for
proposer	* all risks are covered
	* a person who fills in an insurance application form

An insurance broker will be able to advise you about the type of policy you need and which company can provide the best cover.

Most people will at some time have to consider the following kinds of insurance:

Home buildings   Motor cycle or car
Home contents   Life

Home buildings insurance is designed to pay for the complete rebuilding of your house and for repairs. It may cost more to rebuild your house than to buy a similar one. Therefore, you should work out the rebuilding costs very carefully before you arrange any insurance. Here is a way of working out the rebuilding cost of a house.

Rebuilding Costs Guide

1 Work out the total floor area of your property, including garage and upstairs.
2 Find the current cost of rebuilding, presently £40 per square foot. You can check with a local builder.
3 Multiply **1** by **2** = £ sum to be insured.

Exercise 74

Work out the rebuilding cost of this property:

area of house   = 1000 square feet
area of garage = 400 square feet
cost per sq. ft. =   £41.50p

When you decide to insure your home contents you must decide how much it would cost to buy new items. If you do not you may not be able to replace things which are stolen or damaged.

Exercise 75

Use this table to work out the value of items in an average home.

	Hall Landing Living Room	Kitchen	Dining Room	Bedrooms/ Bathroom	Garage/Sheds/ Loft and Other Rooms	TOTAL
(a) household appliances, furniture, carpets, TV and audio equipment						
(b) cutlery, glass, china, clocks, ornaments, pictures, silver						
(c) curtains, household linen, towels						
(d) light fittings, tools, toys and miscellaneous items						
(e) jewellery, watches, furs, cameras, clothing and pedal cycles						

If you do not want to insure your home or its contents no one can force you to. Unless you have a mortgage, then your building society will insist on Home Building insurance. If you buy a motor cycle or car you must insure it. It is a criminal offence to drive any vehicle on the road without insurance.

Basically, there are two types of motor insurance. They are third party insurance and comprehensive insurance.

A **third party** policy only covers damage to other people, their vehicles or property.

A **comprehensive** policy covers you as well as other people. This policy will pay for any damage to your motor cycle or car – a third party policy will not.

Exercise 76

Opposite is a motor insurance proposal form. Fill it in correctly using the details given below. (Your teacher can make a photocopy of this form for you.)

The young man mentioned in the exercise has just bought a Honda 125 motor cycle which is valued at £375.00. The machine is two years old. Its registration number is RAT 123Y. It was bought on 3rd July.

The young man is David James Fox, he lives at 37 Dower Rise, Whitby, North Yorkshire, YO21 1XZ.

David works as an apprentice motor mechanic. He has decided to ask for comprehensive insurance.

He was born on 30th January and is nineteen this year.

David has had insurance for a moped. His policy number was RAC/1234567. It earned him a 40% no claims bonus.

David passed his driving test two months ago. He does not have physical disabilities, nor any convictions for driving offences.

Deciding about life insurance is even more difficult than choosing the right form of cover for your property. Many families have been known to suffer unnecessarily because they failed to consider adequate life insurance.

Life insurance is not just for men, nor simply for wage earners. Wives and mothers need life insurance cover as well.

There are as many life insurance schemes as there are insurance companies. However, there are two main types of life insurance – whole life and endowment.

A **whole life** policy guarantees an income after the death of the person insured.

An **endowment** policy provides cover against death and also gives the proposer a means of saving – providing he services until the policy matures.

Example

If an endowment policy is for £10,000 over fifteen years, the proposer will receive the sum of £10,000 at the end of the fifteen-year period. If the proposer dies before maturity his estate is paid the same sum.

Exercise 77

Complete the proposal for life insurance on pages 34 and 35. Use your own name, address and health details, but imagine that you are married with two children aged 7 and 4.

Exercise 78

Use your local telephone directory to find the names and addresses of insurance companies and brokers.

Choose a broker and write a letter asking for some information about home contents insurance.

SOUTH RIDING MOTOR INSURANCE

Proposal for motor insurance
Please answer all questions fully, leave no blanks. Use black ink.

The proposer should read the accompanying notes for guidance before completing this proposal form.
Please use block capitals in the interests of clarity and efficiency.

PROPOSER
Surname _____
Other name(s) _____
Address _____
_____
_____
_____
Postcode _____
Date of birth _____

Details of vehicle

Make/Description of vehicle	Year of reg.	cc	value
Registration	Date acquired	cost	

Cover required

Comprehensive Third party	Duration of policy	Number of any other policy	Number of other vehicles

Answer all of the following questions as accurately as possible. Incorrect answers may invalidate your insurance should you make a claim.

Have you previously been refused insurance? YES/NO
If YES, by whom were you refused? _____
Will your vehicle be driven by any other person? YES/NO
Give name(s) of other drivers if YES _____
Do you hold a full driving licence? YES/NO
Period, in years and months, full licence has been held ____ years ____ months
Do you have any physical disabilities or defective eyesight? YES/NO
Have you been convicted of any driving offence during the last ten years? YES/NO
Give details if YES _____
_____
_____

Declaration   I declare that to the best of my knowledge all of the statements on this proposal for insurance are true and complete and I have not witheld any vital information. I agree that this proposal shall be the basis of any contract.

Signature _____
Date _____

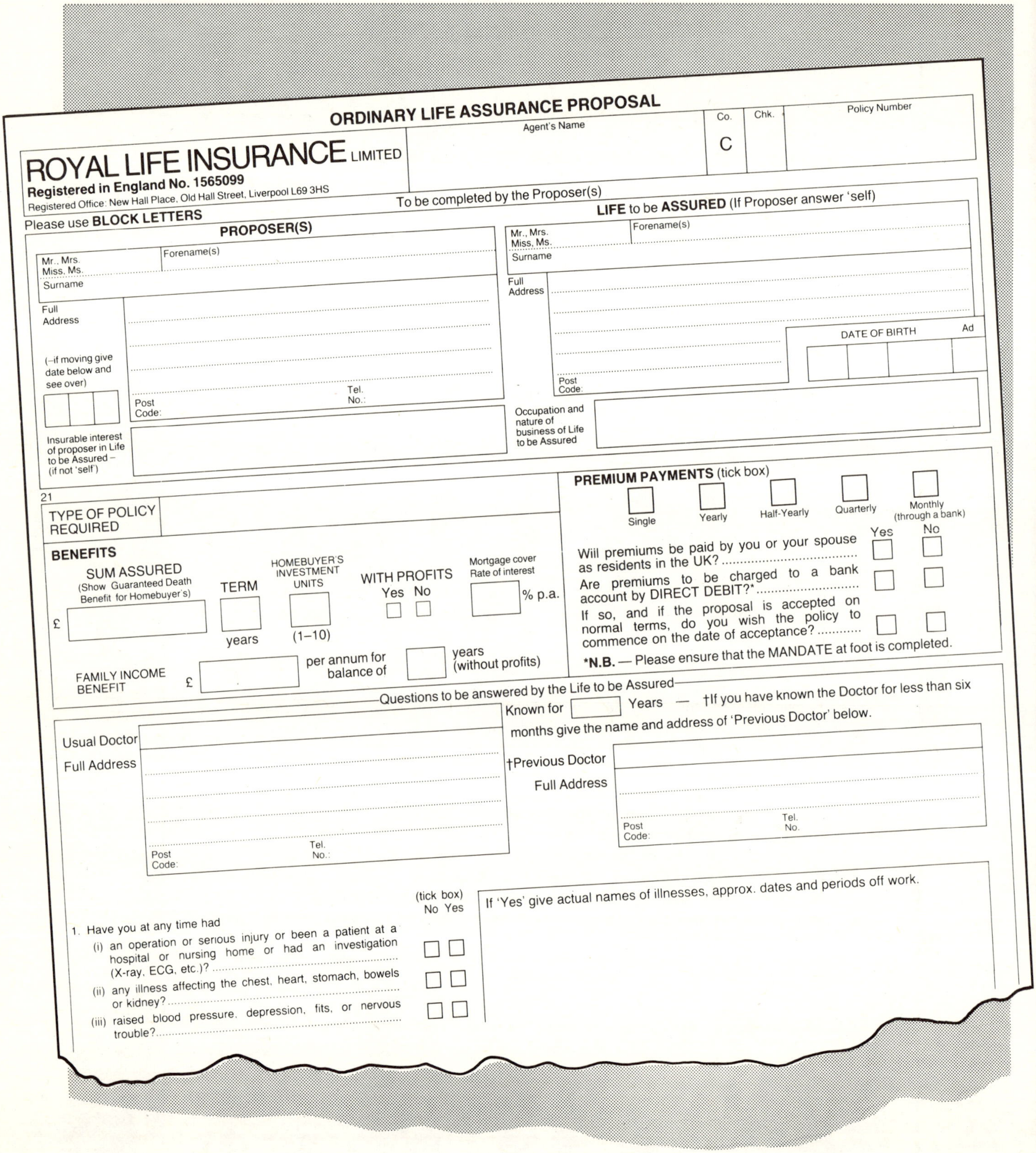

ORDINARY LIFE ASSURANCE PROPOSAL

		Co.	Chk.	Policy Number
Agent's Name		C		

ROYAL LIFE INSURANCE LIMITED
Registered in England No. 1565099
Registered Office: New Hall Place, Old Hall Street, Liverpool L69 3HS

To be completed by the Proposer(s)

Please use **BLOCK LETTERS**

PROPOSER(S)

Mr., Mrs. Miss, Ms.

Forename(s)

Surname

Full Address

(—if moving give date below and see over)

Post Code:

Tel. No.:

Insurable interest of proposer in Life to be Assured — (if not 'self')

21

LIFE to be ASSURED (If Proposer answer 'self')

Mr., Mrs. Miss, Ms.

Forename(s)

Surname

Full Address

Post Code:

DATE OF BIRTH

Ad

Occupation and nature of business of Life to be Assured

TYPE OF POLICY REQUIRED

PREMIUM PAYMENTS (tick box)

Single   Yearly   Half-Yearly   Quarterly   Monthly (through a bank)

BENEFITS

SUM ASSURED (Show Guaranteed Death Benefit for Homebuyer's)	TERM	HOMEBUYER'S INVESTMENT UNITS	WITH PROFITS Yes No	Mortgage cover Rate of interest
£	years	(1–10)		% p.a.

FAMILY INCOME BENEFIT £ _____ per annum for balance of _____ years (without profits)

Will premiums be paid by you or your spouse as residents in the UK? ....

Are premiums to be charged to a bank account by DIRECT DEBIT?* ....

If so, and if the proposal is accepted on normal terms, do you wish the policy to commence on the date of acceptance? ....

Yes   No

***N.B.** — Please ensure that the MANDATE at foot is completed.

Questions to be answered by the Life to be Assured

Known for _____ Years — †If you have known the Doctor for less than six months give the name and address of 'Previous Doctor' below.

Usual Doctor

Full Address

Post Code:

Tel. No.:

†Previous Doctor

Full Address

Post Code:

Tel. No.:

(tick box) No Yes

If 'Yes' give actual names of illnesses, approx. dates and periods off work.

1. Have you at any time had
   (i) an operation or serious injury or been a patient at a hospital or nursing home or had an investigation (X-ray, ECG, etc.)? ....
   (ii) any illness affecting the chest, heart, stomach, bowels or kidney? ....
   (iii) raised blood pressure, depression, fits, or nervous trouble? ....

2. Are you now under medical care, receiving treatment, taking pills or medicine or on a special diet or under supervision at a hospital or clinic? .... ☐ ☐

3. Have you seen a doctor in the last 5 years for any ailment or treatment other than above? .... ☐ ☐

4. Do you intend to travel or reside abroad, engage in any hazardous pursuit, fly other than as a fare paying passenger or fly over 10,000 miles in any year? .... ☐ ☐

5. Has any life assurance proposal on your life been postponed, declined, withdrawn or accepted on special terms? .... ☐ ☐

6. Are any of your parents, brothers or sisters dead? .... ☐ ☐

If 'Yes' give full details.

If 'Yes', state:
Relationship   Age at Death   Cause

Height	ft.	ins.	Weight (in indoor clothes)	st.	lbs.

ALL BENEFITS AND PREMIUMS PAYABLE IN THE U.K. IN STERLING

I have read the NOTES ON COMPLETION overleaf and declare that to the best of my knowledge and belief the above information is true and complete. I, the Life to be Assured, consent to the Company seeking medical information from any doctor who at any time has attended me concerning anything which affects my physical or mental health or seeking information from any insurance office to which a proposal has been made for insurance on my life and I authorise the giving of such information.

Signature of Life to be Assured
(and Proposer if the same)

Signature of Proposer(s)
(if other than Life to be Assured)

Date:

Date:

DIRECT DEBITING MANDATE

I/We authorise you until further notice in writing to charge to my/our account with you, unspecified amounts which may be debited thereto at the instance of the ROYAL LIFE GROUP by direct debit.

POLICY NUMBER | Co. **C** | Chk. |

Name of account to be debited

Bank Account Number

Bank Sorting Code

Please insert Full Postal Address of **BANK** in Block Capitals

THE MANAGER
....
....
....

Signature

Date

Note for the Bank:—

ADDRESS FOR CORRESPONDENCE – PLEASE QUOTE POLICY NUMBER
Royal Life Insurance Ltd.,
Input Department,
P.O. Box 140,
New Hall Place, Liverpool L69 3EU

Banks may decline to accept instructions to charge Direct Debits to certain types of accounts other than current accounts.

SEE OVERLEAF FOR FURTHER INFORMATION

306L

Building Societies and Mortgages

MORTGAGES AVAILABLE

★ UP TO 100% FOR SUITABLE APPLICANTS
★ UP TO 3¼ × SALARY IF REQUIRED
★ NORMAL INTEREST RATES
★ ALSO AVAILABLE FOR COUNCIL HOUSE PURCHASE AND REMORTGAGES

Few people have sufficient money to be able to pay cash for a house or flat, so they borrow. Most borrowers arrange a house buying loan through a building society or a bank.

This type of loan is called a mortgage. The borrower agrees to hand over the property to the lender if the loan is not repaid in an agreed amount of time.

A building society or bank will probably agree to lend a house buyer about 80% of the purchase price of his house. The buyer will have to provide the other 20% himself.

A mortgage can last for twenty or thirty years. During that time the borrower makes a monthly repayment of loan and interest on the loan. The building societies get the money to lend house buyers from people who want to save; the saver is paid interest on the money in his account. This interest is less than the borrower pays the building society.

Investment Interest Rates - with the Woolwich!

	Interest rate per annum	Gross equivalent with income tax at 30%
Share Accounts Minimum £1. Invest or withdraw when you like, at any Woolwich branch. Interest paid or added half yearly.	7·25%	10·36%
Guaranteed Bonus Shares Minimum £1,000. 1¾% above Share rate, guaranteed for 2 years. Interest added annually. Withdrawals at 90 days notice, with loss of interest.	9·00%	12·86%

*Interest Rates up on these Accounts

	Interest rate per annum	Gross equivalent with income tax at 30%
*Higher Interest Shares Minimum £500. 1% above Share rate, withdrawals at 28 days notice, or immediately with loss of 28 days interest.	8·25%	11·79%
*Monthly Income Shares Minimum £500. For a regular income from your savings at 1% above Share rate. Withdrawals at 28 days notice.	8·25%	11·79%

Read the 'Mortgages Available' advertisement, then answer these questions:

a) How does the amount of loan offered differ from the usual building society mortgage?
b) How much could a person earning £10,000 a year borrow?

Exercise 80

Examine the Woolwich advertisement. Copy out this paragraph about interest rates and fill in the missing words.

The -------- offers four types of s----- account. Each has a different ---- of interest per annum. ---------- ----- ------ pays the highest rate of interest; this is because the saver has to give ------ days notice of a withdrawal and lose -------- . The ----- account allows savers to ------ or -------- whenever they like. This pays the ------ rate of interest as the society is not sure that the ----- will ---- money in the ------- .

MONTHLY INCOME SHARES CONDITIONS OF ISSUE

1. Monthly Income Shares will be investment shares in the Society and holders will be members of the Society bound by its Rules and these Terms of Issue.

2. The minimum holding will be £500. The maximum holding will be in accordance with the limitation on overall holdings from time to time in force.

3. Interest will be at the rate payable from time to time on the Society's ordinary Share Account plus a variable premium. Notice of any variation in this premium rate will be by advertisement in accordance with the Society's rules. Interest will be payable from the day following the Society's receipt of an investment and will be allowed up to and including the day of a withdrawal.

4. Interest in respect of each calendar month will be paid to a bank or giro account or Woolwich Share Account, nominated by the investor(s), by the 15th day of the following month (save that the first payment of interest on an account opened after the 15th day of the month will be made not later than the 15th day of the next month but one after the month in which the account was opened).

5. Subject to the Society's right under Rule 35 to require six months' notice, withdrawals may be made on 28 days notice, in writing, by the investor(s).

6. If the balance on a Monthly Income Share Account falls below £500, the Society reserves the right to transfer the balance to an ordinary Share Account.

7. For each account a passbook will be provided in which all transactions will be recorded. A statement will be sent to the investor(s) each April showing the capital balance at the end of March and the interest paid during the previous year.

Exercise 81

Explain to a partner the way a monthly income share account works.

Wordsearch

All of these words are concerned with money matters, look for them in the wordsearch below.

Net	Inland Revenue
Insurance	Bonus
Gross	Loan
Details	Cheque
Savings	Bank
Statement	Overtime
Credit	Payment
Account	Budget
Financial	Debit
Currency	Deduction
Employee	Signature
Withdrawal	Income
Mortgage	Balance
Instalment	Wages
Cash	Pay

M	B	X	J	E	M	W	V	A	E	V	M	Y	E	B	S	B	K	P
M	O	R	T	G	A	G	E	Y	C	H	S	U	R	K	I	W	S	T
L	V	A	O	M	P	B	J	S	T	A	T	E	M	E	N	T	R	G
I	E	C	N	A	R	U	S	N	I	N	S	T	A	L	M	E	N	T
J	R	U	Y	W	S	D	I	F	N	G	R	O	S	S	E	D	T	R
P	T	K	I	W	U	G	F	W	L	F	N	E	T	U	F	Y	R	K
B	I	S	N	A	N	E	D	I	A	O	P	A	Y	M	E	N	T	U
E	M	F	E	A	O	T	N	T	N	C	A	A	T	B	O	R	U	P
B	E	E	X	G	B	E	I	H	D	A	C	N	Y	U	M	R	S	G
E	U	S	L	I	A	T	E	D	R	E	N	O	N	Q	R	M	G	G
X	A	A	D	N	L	W	Y	R	E	M	D	C	U	X	L	E	E	Q
I	I	V	J	C	A	S	H	A	V	P	E	U	I	N	Y	B	F	X
X	M	I	J	O	N	Y	S	W	E	L	B	R	C	A	T	L	U	X
C	J	N	X	M	C	S	T	A	N	O	I	R	H	T	L	A	P	C
V	P	G	S	E	E	R	F	L	U	Y	T	E	E	L	I	F	H	T
B	C	S	P	R	U	S	E	A	E	E	X	N	Q	E	E	O	U	L
I	S	A	O	Y	Q	H	H	D	C	E	A	C	U	S	H	X	N	T
F	A	Q	D	O	S	A	H	O	I	L	H	Y	E	C	L	M	G	Q
Y	F	U	A	A	V	B	A	B	U	T	F	B	Y	R	W	Q	P	F

Exercise 82

Copy out this passage and fill in the spaces with suitable words.

Budgeting

Most people are very pleased to ------- their first --- packet. It is often the very first time that they have had money to ----- exactly as they want. However, they have to remember that they will have extra -------- to consider. Even if they live at ---- , they will have to pay for their------ . If they have far to go to ---- they will have to pay for --- ----- or some other form of transport.

It is a good idea to put some money ----- to pay for weekly -------- , such as keep, fares, ------------- , clothes and other ------ . This is called budgeting.

Exercise 83

Very few people enjoy paying income tax. Ask some adults for their views on tax. They may like to consider:

    fairness
    types of tax
    income tax inspectors

Use this information which you collect to write a report about attitudes to income tax.

Exercise 84

a) All of these mixed-up words are to do with money matters. Yap = pay.
    Sort out these mixed-up words and write them down.

tideb	qchuee
sitoped	terinset
dertic	cebanal
ouacctn	magorget
arylas	utidecdns

b) Write down a definition of each of the following:

        a cheque
        a current account
        a signature
        a debit
        a credit

Exercise 85

Give a short talk to explain one of the following:

    the need for budgeting
    income tax
    superannuation

6 Take Two Wheels

Mopeds, scooters and motor cycles are a cheap, handy method of getting around. This kind of transport gives a rider lots of freedom. He or she can get out and about without worrying about the time of the last train or bus, or about the cost of a taxi.

Two-wheeled vehicles use much less petrol than cars. Some mopeds claim to do over 200 miles on a gallon of petrol.

They are also easier to park and much quicker to drive around in town – especially when cars are stuck in rush hour traffic jams.

You will soon be old enough to ride some types of motor cycle. This will place a lot of responsibility on you. So, before you go out to buy one, or ride one you should think very carefully about these things:

* what to buy
* where to buy
* how to finance the purchase
* the legal requirements
* special and protective clothing
* training courses

What is a moped?

Exercise 86

In small groups or as a class talk about mopeds and motor cycles, share your knowledge with those who know less about them.

Try to define a moped.
Think about the size of the engine.
Consider speed restrictions.
Are there any other restrictions?
Which type of licence will a rider need?
Anything else?

A moped suitable for a sixteen-year-old, is a motor cycle with an engine capacity of 50cc or less, which is restricted to a speed of 30 mph.

Exercise 87

Look at these pictures of motor cycles and read the information very carefully.

MBX50S

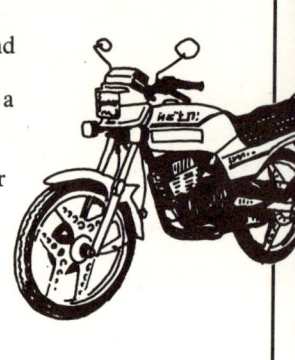

Designed for the sixteen year olds and styled with all the big bike features this attractive sports moped features a high performance two-stroke 49cc engine with 6-speed transmission, Honda's revolutionary Pro-Link rear suspension, 18" wheels and full size frame, new style ComStar wheels, disc front brake, rev counter, twin rear view mirrors and rear carrier. Dimensions are: length 1970mm, width 675mm, height 1000mm with 18" wheels and 12 litre fuel tank.

MTX50S

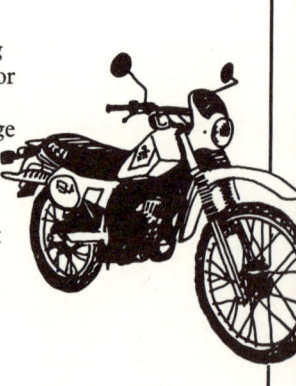

Styled on our championship winning motorcross machines and designed for on-off road dual purpose trail riding the MTX50 offers an exciting package for sixteen year olds. Featuring 49cc two-stroke engine, 6-speed transmission, Pro-Link rear suspension, full size frame, 21" front and 18" rear wheels, high level exhaust, long travel front suspension and rear carrier. Dimensions are: length 2045mm, width 810mm, height 1145mm with a 9.5 litre fuel tank.

Melody

Honda design brings on a new look to scooters. The ever popular Melody comes in many attractive body colours and is available with or without electric starting. Key features include: Fully automatic transmission, 12 volt electrics, front basket and rear carrier, fuel guage and rear view mirror. Dimensions are: length 1520mm, width 630mm, height 960mm with 10" front and rear wheels and a 3.2 litre fuel tank.
Deluxe model available with electric starter and legshield pocket.

a) Which motor cycle would suit a young man who had to travel to work along a farm track as well as on the road?
b) Which model would be best for a young person who worked in an office or shop?
c) If you could, which one would you buy?

d) Write a story in which two friends talk about motor cycles. One could explain to the other which type of bike is best for an urban traveller, and which is really for fun.

The two most popular ways of buying a moped or a motor cycle are:
1 from a motor cycle dealer
2 privately, through the classified advertisements in a local newspaper

Exercise 88

Read this classified advertisement reproduced below. Compare it with that for the 'Melody'.

> **Suzuki 50.** Ex.cond, Xreg. Taxed/tested Dec. £125 ono. Tel:0482-973123 after 6pm.

a) Which advertisement gives the buyer the most information?
b) Is there anything on the 'Melody' advertisement that you do not need to know?
c) Make a list of the advantages and disadvantages of each method of buying.
d) Which do you think will be the safer way of buying a motor cycle?
e) Talk about your answers with a partner. Have either of you got an answer which the other hasn't. Is it important?

Exercise 89

Read through this passage at least twice, and then talk about it with a partner. Copy it out and fill in the gaps with suitable words.

Your local motor cycle d----- will be able to help you to choose the best m----. If you only want one to go sh------, then a ----- with a c------ b----- is essential. The sc----- style models give better protection in b-- w------, if that is important to you. Also your local dealer can help you with any q-------- about tr------, i--------, cl----ng and accessories. He may also be able to help with a l-- i------- finance scheme.

Your motor cycle club has decided to produce a guide for prospective motor cycle buyers. Your share of the work is to classify this list of dealers according to place of business.

List these dealers in alphabetical order of their address.

Motor Cycle Dealers

Baker Cyril, 59 Trinity la, Beverley . . . . Hull 881244
C.E.BARNES LTD.

> INC: LEN HALL (MOTORCYCLES)
> MOTOR CYCLE DEALERS
> HONDA PUCH N.V.T.
> Repairs and Spares
>
> 453 Holderness rd   Hull 74400
> Hull

Barton Frank, 2-4 Popple st . . . . Hull 25655
Blakey K,
  17 Walton st . . . . Hull 508955
  Do. . . . . Hull 563703
Bol d'Or of Hull,George st . . . . Hull 224736
Brentano C.P, 19 St. Nicholas rd, Beverley . . . . Hull 882433
Brentano Kenneth E,36 Beckside,Beverley . . . . . Hull 862413
Burton Robin Ltd, York rd Garage, Beverley . . . . Hull 867189
Eagle Motorcycles (Beverley)
  11 Flemingate,Beverley. . . . . Hull 867618
FIVEWAYS MOTORCYCLES

> DISCOUNT YAMAHA CENTRES
> NORTH HUMBERSIDES
> ONLY 100% YAMAHA
> SPECIALIST DEALER
>
> Clothing Spares Helmets Accessories etc
>
> 141 Askew av,   Hull 55023
> Near Fiveways Roundabout,Hull
>
> Buying Elsewhere Can Damage Your Wealth

HARBOUR MOTORS,51/53 Walton st . . . . Hull 55045
HULL MOTORCYCLE CENTRE,
  104 Witham . . . . Hull 225349
  Workshop Reception. Hull 226240

Mayo Robin (Motorcycles),12 Clough rd. . . . . . . Hull 42058

EVERYTHING
for the
MOTORCYCLIST
Main agents on Humberside for
HONDA, YAMAHA, SUZUKI, BULTACO,
MONTESA, VESPA, LAMBRETTA and JAWA/CZ.
Large stock of clothing, spares & accessories

353/359 Anlaby Road, (Boulevard/Selby Street Corner), Hull.
Tel: **23529**
Spares Hotline: **24745**

Myers & Marshall, 151 Spring Bank . . . . Hull 228232
Neval Motorcycles Ltd
  58 Holderness rd . . . . Hull 24867
PETERS OF HULL,184-188 Beverley rd
  Sales & Service Depts. . . . . Hull 28573
  Spares & Accessory Depts . . . . Hull 24139
Pit Stop Motorcycles,
  251A Anlaby rd. . . . . Hull 224995
PULMAN MOTORCYCLES

> BIKE BREAKERS SHOP-NEW AND
> SECONDHAND SPARES/ACCESSORIES
> Bikes Wanted for Cash-Crashed,Damaged or
> Any Condition.Ring 214733 for Collection
>
> 214 Spring Bank,   Hull 214733
> Hull

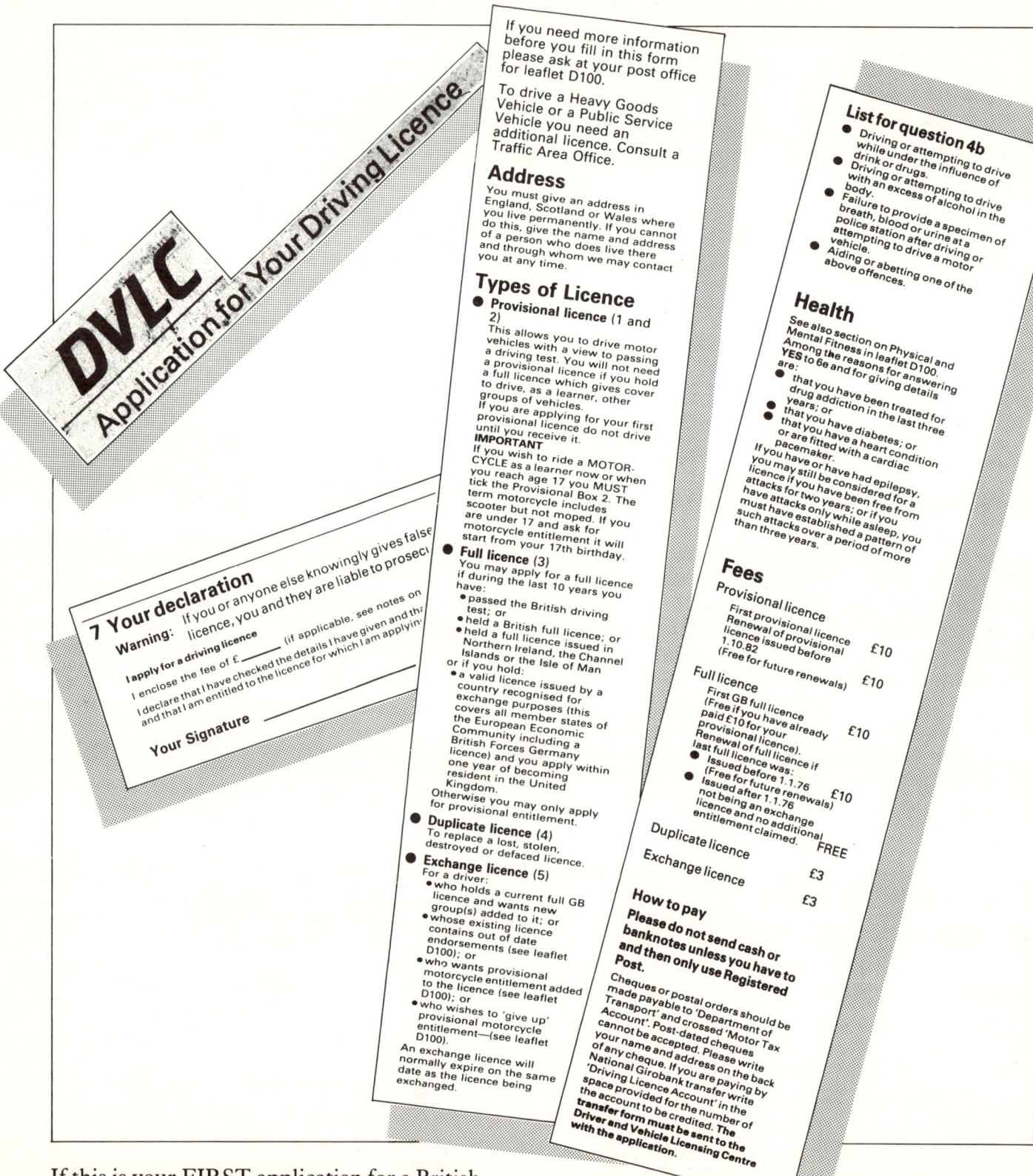

DVLC
Application for Your Driving Licence

If you need more information before you fill in this form please ask at your post office for leaflet D100.

To drive a Heavy Goods Vehicle or a Public Service Vehicle you need an additional licence. Consult a Traffic Area Office.

Address

You must give an address in England, Scotland or Wales where you live permanently. If you cannot do this, give the name and address of a person who does live there and through whom we may contact you at any time.

Types of Licence

● **Provisional licence** (1 and 2)
This allows you to drive motor vehicles with a view to passing a driving test. You will not need a provisional licence if you hold a full licence which gives cover to drive, as a learner, other groups of vehicles.
If you are applying for your first provisional licence do not drive until you receive it.
IMPORTANT
If you wish to ride a MOTOR-CYCLE as a learner now or when you reach age 17 you MUST tick the Provisional Box 2. The term motorcycle includes scooter but not moped. If you are under 17 and ask for motorcycle entitlement it will start from your 17th birthday.

● **Full licence** (3)
You may apply for a full licence if during the last 10 years you have:
● passed the British driving test; or
● held a British full licence; or
● held a full licence issued in Northern Ireland, the Channel Islands or the Isle of Man
or if you hold:
● a valid licence issued by a country recognised for exchange purposes (this covers all member states of the European Economic Community including a British Forces Germany licence) and you apply within one year of becoming resident in the United Kingdom.
Otherwise you may only apply for provisional entitlement.

● **Duplicate licence** (4)
To replace a lost, stolen, destroyed or defaced licence.

● **Exchange licence** (5)
For a driver:
● who holds a current full GB licence and wants new group(s) added to it; or
● whose existing licence contains out of date endorsements (see leaflet D100); or
● who wants provisional motorcycle entitlement added to the licence (see leaflet D100); or
● who wishes to 'give up' provisional motorcycle entitlement—(see leaflet D100).
An exchange licence will normally expire on the same date as the licence being exchanged.

List for question 4b
● Driving or attempting to drive while under the influence of drink or drugs.
● Driving or attempting to drive with an excess of alcohol in the body.
● Failure to provide a specimen of breath, blood or urine at a police station after driving or attempting to drive a motor vehicle.
● Aiding or abetting one of the above offences.

Health

See also section on Physical and Mental Fitness in leaflet D100. Among the reasons for answering **YES** to 6e and for giving details are:
● that you have been treated for drug addiction in the last three years; or
● that you have diabetes; or that you have a heart condition or are fitted with a cardiac pacemaker.
If you have or have had epilepsy, you may still be considered for a licence if you have been free from attacks for two years; or if you have attacks only while asleep, you must have established a pattern of such attacks over a period of more than three years.

Fees

Provisional licence

First provisional licence Renewal of provisional licence issued before 1.10.82 (Free for future renewals)	£10

Full licence

First GB full licence (Free if you have already paid £10 for your provisional licence).	£10
Renewal of full licence if last full licence was:	
● Issued before 1.1.76 (Free for future renewals)	£10
● Issued after 1.1.76 not being an exchange licence and no additional entitlement claimed.	FREE
Duplicate licence	£3
Exchange licence	£3

How to pay

Please do not send cash or banknotes unless you have to and then only use Registered Post.

Cheques or postal orders should be made payable to 'Department of Transport' and crossed 'Motor Tax Account'. Post-dated cheques cannot be accepted. Please write your name and address on the back of any cheque. If you are paying by National Girobank transfer write 'Driving Licence Account' in the space provided for the number of the account to be credited. **The transfer form must be sent to the Driver and Vehicle Licensing Centre with the application.**

7 Your declaration

Warning: If you or anyone else knowingly gives false licence, you and they are liable to prosecu

I apply for a driving licence
I enclose the fee of £_____ (if applicable, see notes on
I declare that I have checked the details I have given and th
and that I am entitled to the licence for which I am applyin

Your Signature

If this is your FIRST application for a British Driving licence, please send this form to:

First Application Section, DVLC, SWANSEA. SA99 1AB.

OTHERWISE, send it to: Driver Licence Section, DVLC, SWANSEA. SA99 1AB.

Opposite you can see some parts of a Driving Licence Application form. Read the notes which are designed to help you.

Exercise 90

Use a dictionary to help you to match the words in column **A** with the meanings in **B**.

A	B
valid	* copied exactly from an original
cardiac	* made so it cannot be read
provisional	* to do with the heart
epilepsy	* living in
resident	* for the time being only
defaced	* can be legally used
duplicate	* disease in which a person can become unconscious

Exercise 91

Copy out these sentences and phrases and fill in the gaps with suitable words from the application form.

a) Cheques and p----- ------ should be made payable to 'Department of ---------'.

b) A d-------- licence costs ----- ------.

c) A ---- licence costs --- ------.

d) If you are applying for a p---------- licence do not ----- until you receive it.

e) The term motor cycle includes s------- , but not ------ .

Exercise 92

What is said on the form about:
a) drug addiction?
b) post-dated cheques?
c) National Girobank transfers?
d) being asleep?
e) cash or banknotes?
f) first applications for a licence?

Exercise 93

a) Imagine that you have suffered from epilepsy in the past, but you have not had an attack for five years. If you apply for a driving licence will you be issued with one? If you answer 'yes' explain why.

b) If you need more information before filling in the Application for a Driving Licence, which leaflet should you read and where can you get one?

c) When will a business, club or hotel address be accepted as your permanent address?

d) What should you do if you do not have a permanent address in England, Scotland or Wales?

Exercise 94

Here is the first section of a Driving Licence application form.

Please complete this form in **BLACK INK** and **BLOCK LETTERS**

1 About yourself

a. Surname — Name of person who applies

Christian or forenames

Please tick box or state other title such as Dr. Rev.

b. Mr [1] Mrs [2] Miss [3]

Other title

Your full permanent address in Great Britain (see note on left)

c. Number and Road / The address of

District or Village / the place where

Post Town / you normally live

Postcode (Your licence may be delayed if the postcode is not quoted)

d. Please tick box — Male [1] Female [2]

e. Please give your date of birth — Day Month Year

f. Have you ever held a British licence (full or provisional)? Answer **YES or NO**

If YES please enter your Driver Number (if known) in the box below (and make a separate note of it).

a) What may happen if you leave the postcode off your address?

b) Find out what else you will need before you can ride a motor cycle on a road.

Exercise 95

a) On the next page is a proposal form for a motor cycle insurance policy. Write down the answers to questions **1** to **12**.

b) What will third party insurance cover?

As a learner rider (with a provisional licence) you have to display L-plates on your bike. You must also wear a safety helmet.

THE D.A. MOTOR CYCLE SCHEME

PROPOSAL FOR MOTOR CYCLE INSURANCE

Under the special scheme operated at the request of The Motor Agents' Association
by Devitt (D.A. Insurance) Limited, and underwritten by The H.P. Motor Policies at Lloyd's.

MATERIAL FACTS	**IMPORTANT** — In your own interest it is essential that you disclose all material facts that may be likely to influence acceptance of the proposal or the assessment of the premium, otherwise your contract of insurance could be made void. For instance, a condition such as vertigo which is not specified in question 8 is a material fact which must be disclosed. If you are in doubt whether a fact is material or not, disclose it for your own protection.

Please answer all questions. Blanks or dashes are not acceptable.

1. Proposer's details: State Title Mr /Mrs /Miss /

Surname ....

First Names ....

Address ....

....

Post Code ....

Age last birthday .... Date of birth ....

State type of insurance cover required   Comprehensive/Third Party Fire and Theft/
(Delete as appropriate)   Third Party Only/Fire and Theft Only

Give details of your licence   (i) Full/Provisional/International/No licence
(Delete as appropriate)   (ii) Current/Expired/Disqualified?
and state
how long you have been driving a motor cycle .... years .... months

Country of origin ....

Occupation (If unemployed, give nature of normal employment)

Full Time ....

Part time ....

NOTE: Use for despatch, courier or messenger services is excluded.

2	Make of Motor Cycle	Model (state if sidecar is attached)	Cubic capacity	Year of Manufacture	Registration Mark	Value including accessories	Total value of accessories

3   Are there any accessories fitted? If so, list items and values.
(Note: Accessories not permanently attached to the motor cycle, helmets and clothing are not covered by this insurance)   YES NO ....
....

4   Are there any alterations from the standard model, for example, customisation, modifications or special paint finishes? If yes, give details   YES/NO

5   Is the motor cycle normally kept in a locked garage overnight? If not, give details of parking arrangements   YES NO

6   Is cover required for additional driver/s? If yes, give names. **(Note: that a separate proposal form must be completed and attached in respect of each additional driver.)**   YES/NO

7   Have you lived continuously in the United Kingdom for the last three years?   YES NO

8   Have you any physical defect or infirmity, diabetes, epilepsy or heart condition? If yes, give full details including methods of control   YES/NO

9   Have you had any accidents, losses or thefts in respect of any motor vehicle during the last 3 years? If so, give date and full details of each incident describing the circumstances and stating costs involved.   YES/NO

10   In connection with the driving of a motor vehicle

    (a) have you been convicted of any offence during the last 5 years? If so, give endorsement offence code, date and amount of fine   YES NO

    (b) do you have a prosecution or prosecutions pending? If so, give date and nature of alleged offence   YES NO

11   Have you passed a course of motor cycle training? If so, give name of course and stage passed **(Note: A premium discount may be allowed if a copy of your RAC/ACU or STEP intermediate or advanced pass certificate is attached).**   YES NO

12   Give name of insurance company and full details if in the last five years

    (a) you have been refused insurance in respect of a motor vehicle   YES NO

    (b) you have been required to agree to special terms or conditions such as a compulsory excess or a premium loading   YES NO

    (c) you have been insured in respect of a motor vehicle **(Attach proof of any No Claim Bonus)**   YES NO

I declare that to the best of my knowledge and belief the above statements and particulars are true, that the motor cycle described is my property, or hired to me under a hire purchase agreement and is in good condition, and I hereby agree that this declaration shall be held to be promissory, and so form the basis of the contract between me and the underwriters of The H.P. Motor Policies at Lloyd's, and I am willing to accept a contract of insurance subject to the terms, exceptions and conditions prescribed by the underwriters therein, and to pay a premium thereon **Whether or not this proposal has been completed by me, I confirm that I have read the statements contained therein and accept full responsibility for them.**

A copy of the contract of insurance will be available on request to your agent   Signed .... Date .... 19......

NOTE: Please ask Agent for details of compulsory excesses which apply on all contracts other than third party only.

NOTE TO AGENTS	Agents must NOT without prior consent from the Underwriters issue cover notes to persons who have been convicted of dangerous or drunken driving or taking a vehicle without the owner's consent, or who suffer from diabetes, epilepsy or a heart condition. In order to obtain such consent, this form, together with full details, should be sent for consideration by the Underwriters to DEVITT (D.A. INSURANCE) LIMITED. **The Underwriters reserve the right to decline any proposal.**

Suitable Clothing

A good safety helmet is both a legal requirement and a sensible idea. There are two types of helmet, the open-faced helmet and the full-faced helmet. The open-faced is usually lighter and cheaper than a full-faced helmet. The full-faced helmet offers more facial and weather protection, but is usually heavier.

Whatever style and price of helmet you buy, do make sure that you try the helmet on before you leave the shop. A helmet must fit snugly and be comfortable with a chin strap correctly fastened. If not, it may move around your head and limit your vision.

It is also a good idea to buy waterproof and wind proof clothing. There are many different kinds of suit, jacket and trousers available.

It is very important to keep you hands warm because a loss of feeling in your fingers can mean poor control of your bike. Therefore, a pair of warm gloves are essential.

Riding Lessons and Training

Training makes good sense, there are many useful things which you can learn – these will help you ride more safely. Learning to ride a moped or motor cycle properly can be good fun.

The best place to go to find out about training is the local Road Safety Officer. There will be one at your council offices. He will be able to tell you all about local training and testing centres.

Your local motor cycle dealer may deliver your machine to the local training centre for you. Then you will be able to have basic instruction before you ride on a road.

Useful Riding Tips

* Read the handbook before riding your machine.
* Be sure that you know where the brakes are, how the horn and lights work before you go on the road.
* Be sure that your mirrors are properly adjusted.

* Learn how the throttle works. Turning it towards you makes the machine go faster, turning it away from you helps to slow a machine down.
* Always apply both brakes evenly and firmly.
* Never use the back brake by itself. In wet weather, this can cause a skid.
* Check that all your lights are working and that your tyres are in good condition, each day.
* Whenever you buy petrol, check your tyre pressures.
* If you carry any bags make sure that the weight is evenly distributed.
* Learn the Highway Code.
* Always signal properly and in good time.
* If you park on a hill, point the machine uphill for stability.
* Always lock your machine when you leave it.

Exercise 96

a) What happens when you turn the throttle towards you?
b) Why should you never use the back brake by itself?
c) What should you do each day before you ride your bike?
d) When should you check your tyre pressure?
e) If you carry luggage, what should you do with it?

Exercise 97

Choose a topic from the Highway Code and use it to prepare a short talk to give to your class.

Exercise 98

Write a letter to a friend or relative who is thinking of buying a moped. Advise them of the correct way to set about buying one.

Wordsearch

All of these words are concerned with motor cycles and mopeds, look for them in the wordsearch below.

Epilepsy	Fuel
Gallon	Helmet
Scooter	Maximum
Training	Restricted
Classified	Application
Registered	Comprehensive
Advertisement	Seventeenth
Provisional	Motorcycle
Licence	Transport
Resident	Handbook
Driver	Valid
Petrol	Rider
Weatherproof	Insurance
Duplicate	Defaced
Legal	Moped

```
L R E D I R E V I R D E F A C E D K X
S E I R W M D P G Q E Q O N S R L Q C
J B U G N I N I A R T T A H E L M E T
D E I F I S S A L C C R E T F A G I D
D H T Q I M L L L O I O C N O G U K R
V M U M I X A M O M R P N E O E A Q D
C L O R T E P D N P T S A E R L V S G
P E X R G P P U V R S N R T P C V I A
E C N E C I L P A E E A U N R Y G J A
M L T S M L I L L H R R S E E C E O N
R O K I T E C I I E E T N V H R W V B
V O O D A P A C D N G P I E T O Q H U
R V O E N S T A J S I R L S A T W M X
U E B N K Y I T G I S P Q C E O P X Y
D F D T E X O E C V T Y E O W M F O Q
O X N K R F N X X E E I L O N O E L G
Q L A N O I S I V O R P V T J P B N O
H C H V G M T V Y C E B B E K E S I T
I W H I U P F E G Y D A J R F D L T G
```

Motor cycles

Motor cycles are very manoeuverable in traffic, they are better than cars for urban travel and they take up far less parking space. The chief drawback is, that, they can only carry two people unless a sidecar is fitted. The sidecar reduces speed and manoeuverability.

It has to be said that motor cycles are the most dangerous form of transport used on our roads. Far more motor cycle riders are killed and seriously injured each year than any other type of road user. If you become a motor cycle rider, you must, for your own sake, learn to ride it properly and follow the Highway Code.

More young motor cycle riders are killed and injured than older riders. It may be a good idea to think about this fact and try to come up with an explanation for it.

Motor cycles use petrol engines of various kinds, from the single cylinder 49cc up to the four cylinder 1000cc and larger machines. The normal pattern is for the engine to turn the back wheel by a chain. Some of the larger more complicated machines have a piston drive like a car.

Normally the flow of cold air over and around the engine is used to keep it cool. The engine has ridges or vanes around the outside to make a larger surface area for contact with the air.

Steering is just like a bicycle steering, the handlebars turn the front wheel and the rider leans into the corner as he goes round it.

On the handlebars are all the main controls such as clutch, throttle, front brake and the various gauges which tell the rider about oil, fuel and speed.

The clutch is used to separate the gearbox from the crankshaft so that the rider can change gear easily.

The throttle allows the rider to control the amount of fuel which goes into the engine, so controlling the speed of the motor cycle.

The back brake, gear lever and kick start are all operated by the rider's feet.

7 Sign for This

Signs are a way of giving a message without speaking. They may use words, symbols or pictures, or a mixture of these things to get a message across.

You will see a lot of signs at home, in school or around town, as well as in the countryside. If you cannot read or understand these signs you may get into trouble, get lost or cause an accident.

Example
Look at the motorway sign below.
It gives drivers three important pieces of information:

1 places to which the motorway goes
2 the road to take to get to Nottingham
3 the motorway junction number

The North
Sheffield
Leeds

Nottingham
A 52

25

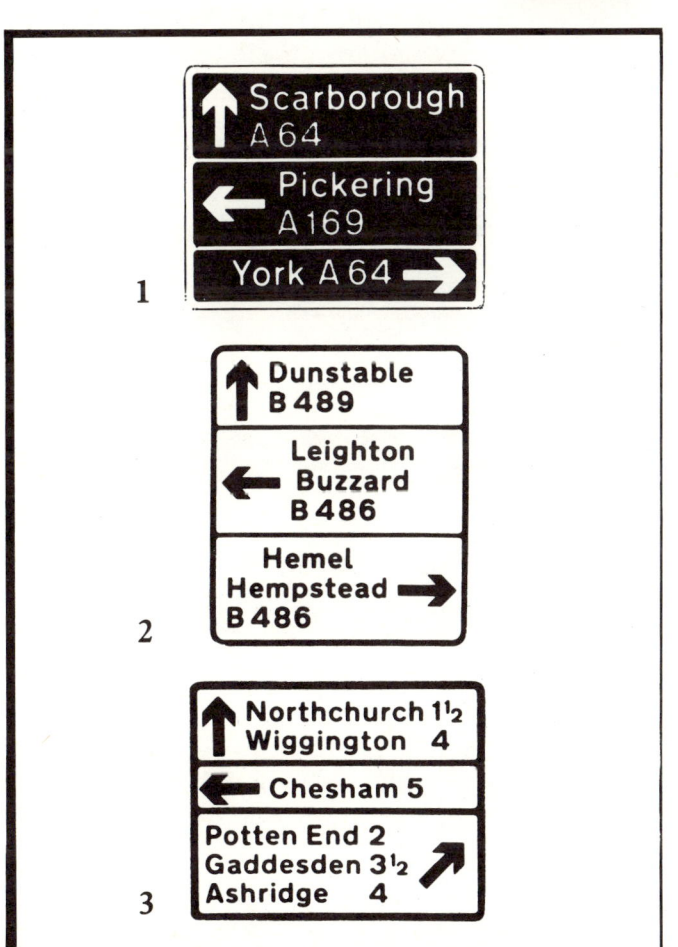

1 Scarborough A 64 / Pickering A 169 / York A 64

2 Dunstable B 489 / Leighton Buzzard B 486 / Hemel Hempstead B 486

3 Northchurch 1½ Wiggington 4 / Chesham 5 / Potten End 2 Gaddesden 3½ Ashridge 4

Exercise 99

Look at the road signs numbered **1**, **2** and **3**.
Write out the answers to these questions:

a) Which road should you take to Pickering?
b) Where will the B489 take you?
c) How far is it to Gaddesden?
d) Which two towns are on the B486?
e) Look carefully at sign 1, if you turn right on the A64, towards which city will you be travelling?
f) How far is Northchurch from Wiggington?
g) Look carefully at sign 3, write out a set of directions for someone who has asked how to get to Ashridge. Remember to tell them how far it is.
h) Find out what colours these signs are from the Highway Code.

As well as telling drivers which road to take, roadsigns tell road users what to do and what not to do. In order to use roads safely you will need to understand these words. You may see many of these words whenever you use the road. Learn them, they will help you to be safe and arrive safely.

Allowed	you may (e.g. parking)
Caution	take care
Construction	building work (e.g. construction work ahead)
Danger	a hazard ahead
Diversion	a change in a route
Exit	way out (e.g. motorway exit)
Look right	look for traffic from the right
Maximum	the highest (e.g. speed)
Prohibited	not allowed (e.g. parking)
Regulations	rules (e.g. motorway)
Subsidence	the road has sunk, often in coal mining areas
Temporary	for a short time only

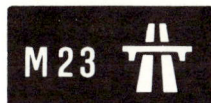 M 23

Motorways are special roads on which the traffic goes fast and straight ahead. Certain types of road users are not allowed to travel on a motorway.

Exercise 100

With a partner work out the answers to these questions:

a) Which of the following vehicles will be allowed on motorways?
    tractors and trailers
    bicycles
    cars
    articulated lorries
    vans
    mopeds
    cars driven by learners

b) Are there any other road users who might not be allowed to use motorways?

c) Write out some reasons for not allowing certain types of traffic on motorways.

Exercise 101

Copy out the following passage from the 'Highway Code' and fill in the spaces with suitable words.

Motorways are dual carriageway roads which must --- be used by p---------- , l------ d------ , c------- and riders of small m---- ------ . Slow-moving vehicles, agricultural v------- and some carriages used by invalids are also prohibited. It is an offence to pick up or set d--- a passenger or a h--------- on any part of a m-------- , including a slip r--- .

Exercise 102

Imagine that you are a policeman, explain to a driver why it is wrong to stop to pick up passengers on a motorway.

Write down the conversation with the policeman.

Exercise 103

Match the words on the left with the meanings on the right:

maximum	not allowed
services	the highest
prohibited	a place to get fuel and food

Some of the signs which you will meet on a motorway may be unfamiliar. These are not the same as ordinary road signs.

Exercise 104

Look carefully at the sequence of signs.

a) What might the figure 50 mean?
b) Why will these signs have flashing lights in the corners?
c) As briefly as you can, explain the meaning of this sequence of signs.

Signs like these above are not found on normal roads, nor are those which follow.

Exercise 105

On some motorways direction signs may be placed over the road, like those below.

a) How may this help drivers?

Read the signs which follow and answer the questions.

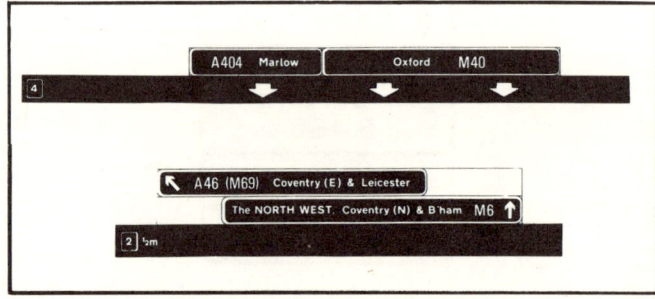

b) Where will the centre lane of the M40 take you?
c) Which road goes to Marlow?
d) What will be the number of the next junction?
e) In which general direction does the M6 go?
f) To which cities does the M6 take you?
g) How far is it to the Coventry (E) junction?

h) If you were driving on the M6 and wanted to go to Leicester, what must you do at the next junction?

Exercise 106

This sign tells drivers that the motorway will end soon. Why is it important to remind drivers that they will leave the motorway soon?

Ordinary roads can be much more complicated than motorways, as this sign shows. Notice that this section of the A4 has three junctions with five destinations marked.

Exercise 107

a) Which road goes to Windsor?
b) Which route will take you to Datchet?
c) To where does the A412 go?
d) Explain why the road to Gerrards Cross has no number.
e) Suggest a reason for writing (B376) in this way.

On ordinary roads you will see a great many signs. They can be divided into three main groups:

    warnings
    orders
    information

Red triangles are warning signs.
Red circles are orders.
Blue squares or rectangles give information.

Traffic signs
SIGNS GIVING ORDERS
These signs are mostly circular and those with red circles are mostly prohibitive

Maximum speed

WARNING SIGNS *Mostly triangular*

Roundabout

This information sign tells lorry drivers which is the best route to take.

Exercise 108

Divide your page into three columns labelled: **orders**, **warnings** and **information**. Carefully examine the road signs below. Decide to which group each belongs and draw it in the correct column.

Remember

   ★ circles give orders/prohibit

      ★ triangles give warnings

R   ★ rectangles give information

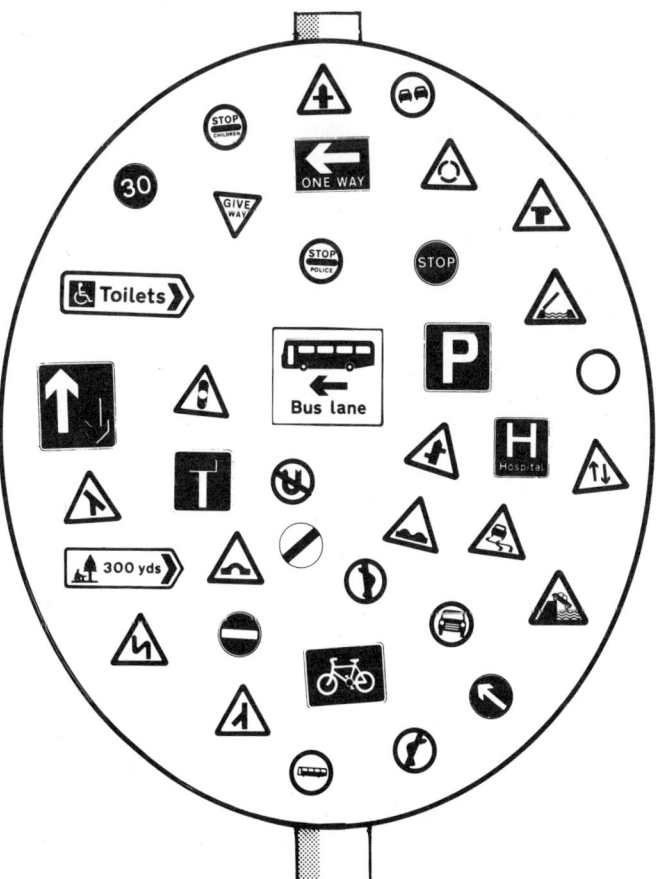

1	a. No Cars or Motorcycles	a. ☐	11	a. Location of Level Crossing without Barrier or Gate	a. ☐
	b. No Motor Vehicles	b. ☐		b. Level Crossing Ahead	b. ☐
	c. Light Vehicles Only	c. ☐		c. Crossroads	c. ☐
2	a. Minimum Speed Limit	a. ☐	12	a. End of Dual Carriageway	a. ☐
	b. Maximum Speed Limit	b. ☐		b. Two-way Traffic Straight Ahead	b. ☐
	c. Advisory Speed Limit	c. ☐		c. No Overtaking	c. ☐
3	a. Low Bridge Ahead	a. ☐	13	a. No Right Turn	a. ☐
	b. Narrow Tunnel	b. ☐		b. No Entry	b. ☐
	c. Hump Bridge	c. ☐		c. Road Turns Sharply	c. ☐
4	a. No Stopping	a. ☐	14	a. Steep Hill Downhill	a. ☐
	b. No Parking	b. ☐		b. Steep Hill Uphill	b. ☐
	c. No Waiting	c. ☐		c. Beware Ramp	c. ☐
5	a. No Cycling	a. ☐	15	a. Repairs	a. ☐
	b. No Cycling or Moped Riding	b. ☐		b. Restaurant	b. ☐
	c. Cycles and Mopeds Only	c. ☐		c. Ring Road	c. ☐
6	a. Hump Back Bridges	a. ☐	16	a. Dual Carriageway Ends	a. ☐
	b. Uneven Road	b. ☐		b. Road Narrows	b. ☐
	c. Hilly Area Ahead	c. ☐		c. One-way Traffic	c. ☐
7	a. One Way	a. ☐	17	a. Pedestrian Crossing	a. ☐
	b. Turn Left Ahead	b. ☐		b. Pedestrian Footpath	b. ☐
	c. Turn Left	c. ☐		c. Entrance to School	c. ☐
8	a. Loose Chippings	a. ☐	18	a. Two-way Traffic Ahead	a. ☐
	b. Uneven Surface	b. ☐		b. End of One-way System	b. ☐
	c. Pot Holes	c. ☐		c. Two-way Traffic Crosses One-way Road	c. ☐
9	a. Slippery Road	a. ☐	19	a. Sharp Deviation	a. ☐
	b. Double Bend	b. ☐		b. Count-down Markers	b. ☐
	c. Bends in Road	c. ☐		c. Turn Left One-way Only	c. ☐
10	a. No Parking	a. ☐	20	a. Start of Motorway	a. ☐
	b. No Overtaking	b. ☐		b. Low Bridge	b. ☐
	c. Priority over Traffic	c. ☐		c. Dual Carriageway	c. ☐

Exercise 109

Each of the above traffic signs has three suggested meanings alongside. Answer all twenty questions by writing down number and letter for the correct meaning (e.g. 1c, if you think c is correct).

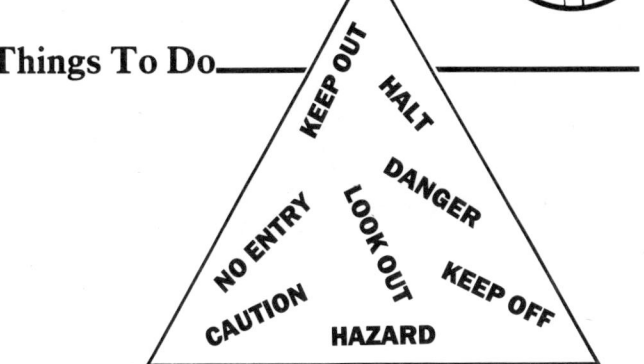

Exercise 110

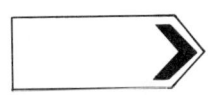

This shaped sign gives information. What do each of these signs tell you?

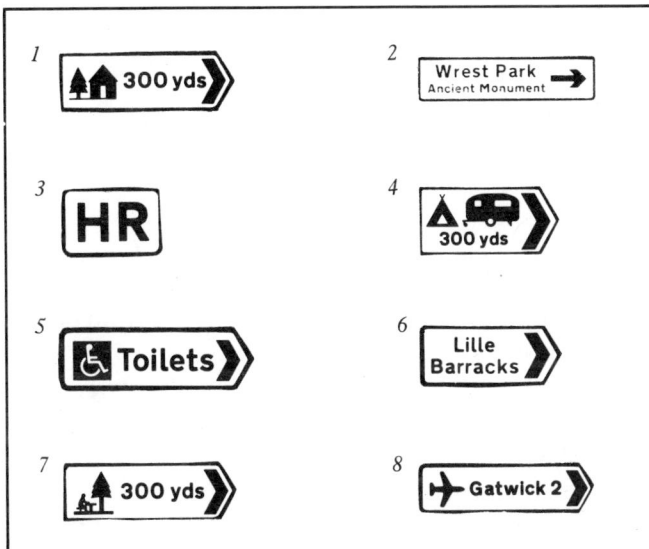

1. 🏠 300 yds
2. Wrest Park Ancient Monument →
3. HR
4. ⚠ 300 yds
5. ♿ Toilets
6. Lille Barracks
7. 🏕 300 yds
8. ✈ Gatwick 2

Exercise 111

All of the signs below were seen on a **1** trip, from **2** to the seaside resort of **3**. Use the signs to tell a story about the trip.

1. (bus)
2. (children crossing)
3. ↑ Scarborough A64
4. (lorry)
5. POISON
6. (level crossing)
7. (falling rocks)
8. (roadworks)
9. (cattle)
10. (low flying aircraft)
11. (wild horses)
12. (wild deer)
13. 🏕 300 yds
14. (steam train)
15. 20%
16. P
17. ℹ Tourist information

Things To Do

All of the words in the triangular sign above are warnings. Some of them warn of a danger, others warn you not to do something.

(Triangle contains: KEEP OUT, HALT, DANGER, KEEP OFF, HAZARD, LOOK OUT, CAUTION, NO ENTRY)

Exercise 112

a) Draw a warning sign which shows a danger.
b) Design a warning sign which shows that a driver must look out for old people crossing a road.
c) Draw a sign that warns that is dangerous to enter a place because of wild animals.

Exercise 113

You will see many signs around your home, in towns and in the countryside, which use these words. Use a dictionary to find the meaning of each word, then write a separate sentence using each word.

vehicles	litter
illegal	meter
pedestrian	trespass
public	roadworks
steep	clearway

Exercise 114

Imagine the following situation. Your school is situated on a busy dual carriageway in a big town. There is a crossroads only one hundred metres to the left of the school. Fifty metres left of the school the 30mph zone ends. A lot of drivers start to accelerate up to 40mph as they pass the school gates. There have been many accidents and near misses outside the school.

Write a letter to your local safety officer. Explain the situation to him and ask what can be done to improve safety.

This sign may be found on many items in shops. It is called the kite-mark. It is a sign of reliability and quality. Products carrying this sign are tested by the British Standards Institution. You should look for it on cots, paint, car windscreens and seat belts.

Why do customers need to be protected by signs?

The previous five signs all guarantee the quality of an item. The Design Centre Label tells shoppers that an article is well designed. Look for it on furniture, cutlery, toys and many other household goods.

Exercise 115

Explain why a potential buyer needs to know that items such as crash helmets and cots are safe to use.

These signs are used on gas fires, cookers, fridges and boilers to show that they are safe.

Many electrical appliances will have this sign stamped on them or attached. It is the B.E.A.B. safety mark. Look for it on cookers, hairdriers, irons and kettles.

All of these signs will be on goods which have been carefully tested.

Exercise 116

a) When you go shopping, why is it important to look for goods with these signs?
b) What would you do if a shopkeeper tried to sell an electric kettle without the B.E.A.B. safety mark?
c) Draw the sign you would expect to find on the following items, write by the side what you expect the sign to tell you about the article.

   an electric kettle
   a gas cooker
   a dining table and chairs
   a Shetland jumper
   a tweed jacket

Exercise 117

Design a sign (without words) to show that the following things are safe and of good quality:

   bicycles
   school equipment
   toys
   some other everyday items

Write a brief description of your sign, say why you have designed it in the way you have.

Certification Trade Mark

Pure New Wool is a high quality material which can be imitated. When you see this sign on a label, you know that the wool which you are buying is really pure. It does not contain recycled wool, other fibre or additives.

Standard signs have taken the chance out of fabric care. The Home Laundering Consultative Committee (H.L.C.C.) Care Labelling System is widely used in Great Britain and accepted in many other countries.

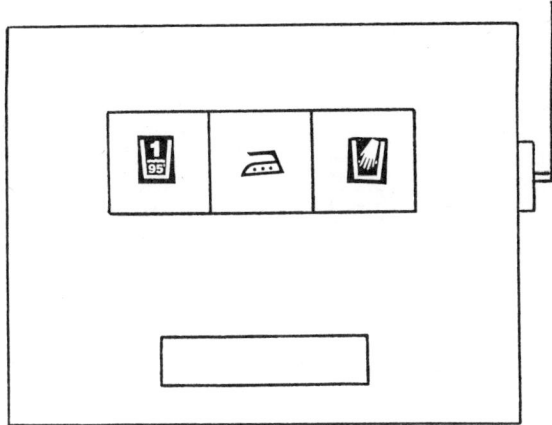

Exercise 118

a) What do you think the three signs above mean?
b) Why are signs better than words for washing instructions?

Exercise 119

Copy this passage and fill in the blanks with suitable words.

Nearly every g------ you buy has a sewn-in label telling you exactly how to w--- it to keep it in the b--- possible condition, according to the f----- it is made from. A garment that is in--------- washed just once can be completely s------ and never restored to g--- condition.

The meaning of some signs is more obvious than others. With a little help and some thought you can work them out. Here are a few tips:

  Triangles are about chlorine bleach.

 Circles tell about dry cleaning.

 Crosses mean *do not*.

Exercise 120

Draw the following signs and write the correct description by the side. This will provide an easy reference guide to the fabric care signs you should find in your clothes.

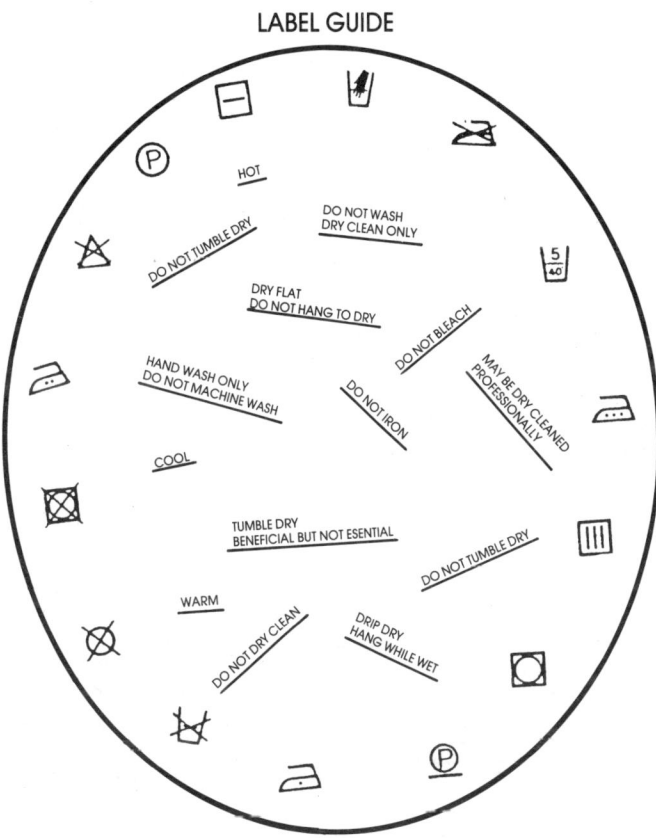

LABEL GUIDE

Here are some words which you will find on clothes' labels. The manufacturers put them there to help you to look after the things you buy. Learn them and be sure that you understand their meaning.

Detergent	washing powder
Dry-cleaning	cleaning without water (it is usually done by special cleaning shops)
Fabric	cloth or material
Non-flammable	will not burn
Permanent press	no need to iron, trousers are often pressed this way
Wring	squeeze water out
Rinse	wash with clean water to remove detergent or soap

Here is a particular washing programme guide from a washing machine users' handbook. Read it carefully. Remember, a garment which is not properly washed may be ruined.

Programme	Max. Load	Dispenser I	Dispenser II	Start position	Energy e	Spin delay	Spin speed	Remarks
[1/95] White cotton (with pre-wash)	4.5 kg 10 lb	✓	✓	A	✓	✓	10	For heavily soiled white cotton articles.
[1/95] White cotton	4.5 kg 10 lb	-	✓	1	✓	✓	10	For normally soiled white cotton articles.
[2/60] Colourfast cotton	4.5 kg 10 lb	-	✓	2	✓	✓	10	Make sure articles are colourfast before washing.
[3/60] White nylon	2 kg 4½ lb	-	✓	3	✓	✓	1-5	For white nylon shirts, overalls, sheets, underwear, etc.
[4/50] Coloured nylon	2 kg 4½ lb	-	✓	4		✓	1-5	For coloured nylon, crimplene, terylene, poly-cotton mixtures,
[5/40] Non-colourfast cottons	4.5 kg 10 lb	-	✓	5	-	✓	10	For coloured cotton items which are colourfast at 40°C but not at 60°C.
[6/40] Delicates (with pre-wash)	1.5 kg 3 lb	✓	✓	C	-	✓	1-3	For heavily soiled acrilan, orlon, courtelle, tricel.
[6/40] Delicates	1.5 kg 3 lb	-	✓	6	-	✓	1-3	For normally soiled acrilan, orlon, courtelle, tricel.
[7/40] Wool (machine washable) and blankets		-	✓	7			1-8	See section "Fabrics"
[9/95] Special finish cottons (with pre-wash)	4.5 kg 10 lb	✓	✓	A	✓	✓	1	Articles capable of being boiled but requiring drip drying
[9/95] Special finish cottons	4.5 kg 10 lb		✓	9	✓	✓	1	Articles capable of being boiled but requiring drip drying
Rinse and spin	4.5 kg 10 lb	-	-	B	-	-	1-10	For rinsing and spinning hand washed articles
[S] Short wash	2 kg 4½ lb		✓	6	-	✓	1-8	For lightly soiled articles

FABRIC CARE GUIDE...For outstanding results...on all temperatures...and on all fabrics.

CODE	1/95	2/60	3/60	4/50	5/40	6/40	7/40	8/30	9/95	HAND WASH ONLY	DO NOT WASH
MACHINE*	Very hot to boil Maximum wash	Hot Maximum wash	Hot Medium wash	Hand-hot Medium wash	Warm Maximum wash	Warm Minimum wash	Warm Minimum wash	Cool Minimum wash	Very hot to boil Medium wash		
HAND WASH	Hand hot (50°C) or boil	Hand hot (50°C)	Hand hot (50°C)	Hand hot	Warm	Warm	Warm Do not rub	Cool	Hand hot (50°C) or boil		
SPIN	Spin or wring	Spin or wring	Cold rinse Short spin or drip-dry	Cold rinse Short spin or drip-dry	Spin or wring	Cold rinse Short spin	Spin Do not hand wring	Cold rinse Short spin	Cold rinse Drip-dry		
FABRICS	White cotton and linen fabrics without special finishes	Cotton, linen or viscose fabrics without special finishes and colour-fast at 60°C.	White nylon: white polyester/cotton fabrics.	Coloured nylon, polyester: cotton and viscose fabrics with special finishes; acrylic cotton fabrics; coloured polyester/cotton fabrics.	Cotton, linen or viscose fabrics with colour fast at 40°C, but not at 60°C.	Acrylics: acetate and triacetate, including mixtures with wool: polyester/wool blends.	Wool, including blankets and wool mixtures with cotton or viscose silk. †Machine washable wool, eg Superwash.	Silk and printed acetate fabrics with colours not fast at 40°C.	Cotton articles with special finishes capable of being boiled but requiring drip-drying.		
PROGRAMME SELECTION	To achieve the best results it is important to select the right programme. If you need to mix different fabric codes in a load, we suggest you combine codes 1 and 2 and wash as 2.					A combination of codes 3 and 4 should be washed as 4. White nylon and fabrics from groups 5-8 should always be washed on their own programme.					

*The terms 'Minimum, Medium and Maximum Wash' refer to the washing time and agitation required. Follow the manufacturer's instructions.

†The International Wool Secretariat recommend Persil Automatic for all Woolmark Superwash woollens.

Woolmark — Pure new wool — Machine washable wool knitwear Superwash

Exercise 121

a) Which fabric would you wash at **1**?

b) How would you wash a blue nylon dress?

c) What does this sign mean: **2**?

d) How would you remove stains from a dress which bore this sign: **3**?

e) How should blankets be washed?

f) **5** is for colour fast fabrics, what does this mean?

g) How does programme **9** differ from **1**?

h) Which fabrics can go in a hot wash?

i) A woollen garment should be washed at **7**, what might happen if you washed a sweater at **2**?

j) If you wanted to wash white and coloured nylon together which programme would you use?

k) Why is it important to select the correct washing programme?

l) Minimum, medium and maximum wash tell us how much w--- and a-------- are needed.

m) If your wash basket contains woollen sweaters, coloured nylon shirts, a silk scarf and a white cotton sheet, which programme should you use?

n) If a garment has lost its label, how could you decide on the correct programme to use?

Exercise 122

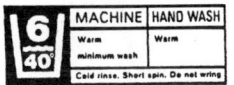 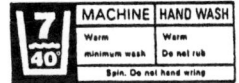

These programmes are very much alike, but they are not the same. What differences are there between programmes **6** and **7**?

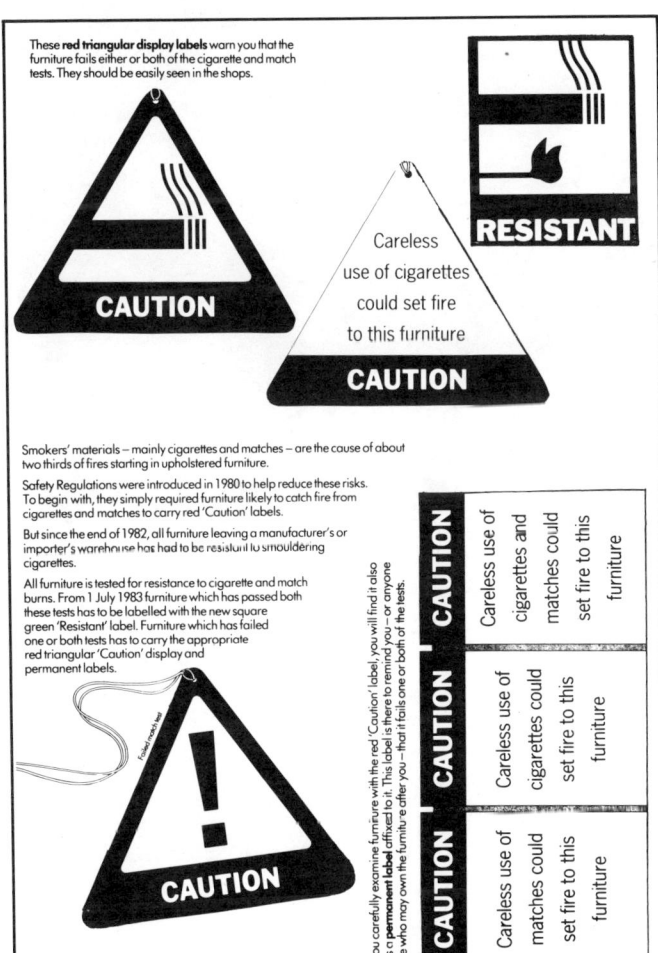

Exercise 123

Use the information about caution labels to help you do one or all of the following.

a) Prepare and give a short talk about caution labels.

b) Write a brief article on caution labels.

c) Write a letter to your local newspaper explaining the improvement and help which these labels give consumers.

Wordsearch

Look for the following words in the wordsearch below:

Highway Code	Chlorine Bleach
Dry Cleaning	Protected
Direction	Quality
Customers	Instructions
Fabric	Traffic Signs
Sequence	Reliability
Motorway	Appliances
Design Council	Garment
Primary Route	Grid
Prohibited	Minimum
Carriageway	Message
Rectangular	Programme
Warning	Passenger
Junction	Guarantee

M	O	T	O	R	W	A	Y	I	V	K	C	Y	N	D	D	E	B	V
E	G	H	S	E	C	N	A	I	L	P	P	A	T	E	E	E	H	F
S	I	V	E	C	U	N	M	L	C	K	T	W	F	T	T	T	Q	S
S	P	M	Q	T	S	T	F	T	H	C	R	E	N	C	I	N	U	F
A	S	G	U	A	T	D	U	V	L	G	A	G	X	E	B	A	A	N
G	H	P	E	N	O	R	E	J	O	D	H	A	T	T	I	R	L	C
E	L	F	N	G	M	Y	Q	S	R	G	I	I	X	O	H	A	I	H
D	Q	W	C	U	E	C	P	R	I	M	A	R	Y	R	O	U	T	E
N	G	W	E	L	R	L	R	R	N	G	W	R	E	P	R	G	Y	C
S	M	H	D	A	S	E	O	O	E	O	N	A	M	C	P	T	X	W
T	U	A	O	R	R	A	G	A	B	L	I	C	R	E	T	B	Q	V
A	M	V	C	O	E	N	R	U	L	P	I	T	O	N	N	I	B	Y
N	I	R	Y	X	G	I	Λ	M	E	Q	T	A	C	U	I	T	O	B
D	N	L	A	F	N	N	M	P	A	E	L	F	B	N	N	N	E	N
A	I	J	W	E	E	G	M	U	C	D	R	A	A	I	U	C	G	P
R	M	R	H	Q	S	J	E	W	H	O	K	B	A	X	L	J	I	C
D	F	C	G	M	S	N	O	I	T	C	U	R	T	S	N	I	H	L
S	O	Y	I	L	A	S	N	G	I	S	C	I	F	F	A	R	T	X
P	J	X	H	J	P	R	I	C	L	F	T	C	Y	P	I	Q	R	Y

53

8 This Year, Something Different

What did you do in your summer holidays last year?

Was everything you did successful?

Did you enjoy every moment?

Are there any activities you would not take part in again?

Exercise 124

Write an account of the way you spent your summer holiday last year.

What would you like to do for your holiday this year?

What do holidays mean to you?

Exercise 125

If you could go any where you chose, where would you like to go and what would you like to do?

Give a short talk about your ideal holiday.

Holidays are often short, but can be very expensive. Therefore, you need to plan them very carefully.

A travel agent can help by offering a ready-made or package holiday, or by making special arrangements according to your instructions.

A travel agent will be able to:
* advise about holidays at home or abroad
* show you brochures and give prices
* make all the necessary arrangements
* obtain travellers cheques and currency
* arrange travel insurance for you and your luggage

If you decide to plan your own holiday and make your own arrangements, you will need to make careful plans.

Exercise 126

a) From the items below, pick out those which are most important to you. You may wish to add other items not shown.
b) Work with a partner. Imagine that you are planning a holiday together. Compare your checklists and pick out those features common to both lists.

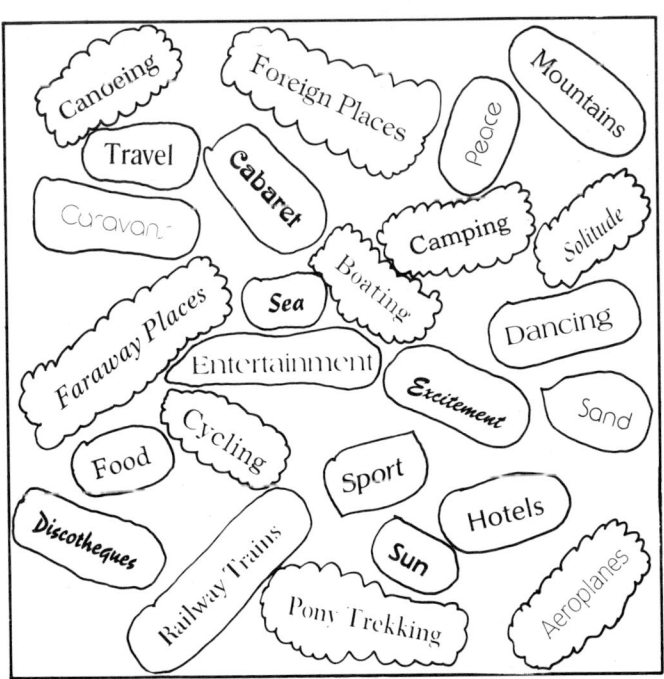

When you are making plans and reading the travel brochures, you may come across some unfamiliar words used in an unusual way.

Exercise 127

Match the words in column **A** with the meanings in **B**.

A		B
inclusive	★	an extra payment
charter	★	everything you have to pay for
surcharge	★	cost of meals and bedrooms
package	★	a travel firm representative who helps you
courier	★	a complete holiday, including fares and hotels
bed & breakfast	★	a flight which carries people at a special price
full board	★	the cost of bedroom and breakfast
booking	★	your reservation
deposit	★	a trip
excursion	★	an amount of money to confirm a booking
supplement	★	an extra payment for better accommodation
itinerary	★	details of holiday and excursions
departure	★	time to leave

The people in your class have probably been to many places at home and abroad. Some may have lived abroad whilst their parents were working.

Exercise 128

a) Make a list of the holiday resorts you have visited in *i)* Britain, and *ii)* in other countries.
b) What was the most exciting thing you saw?
c) Did you eat or drink anything really exciting?
d) How did the weather differ from home?
e) Were there any local specialities to buy?
f) Was there anything you did not like?
g) Write a report based on your answers a) – f). try to bring out special features.

***** For your next task you will need some holiday brochures and an atlas.

Look through the brochures to find holidays and resorts which you like. Use the index in your atlas to find some of the places.

Exercise 129

With a partner, talk about some of the holidays which interest you. You might like to consider some of the following points:

prices	places	activities	plane
car	coach	boat	train
hotel	flat	caravan	camping
entertainment			when

Now write a paragraph about one of the places you would like to visit.

Here is a typical holiday brochure information chart.

DEPARTURES	10 DAYS	17 DAYS	DEPARTURES ON OR BETWEEN							
			1 MAY TO 26 MAY	27 MAY TO 16 JUNE	17 JUNE TO 30 JUNE	1 JULY TO 14 JULY	15 JULY TO 7 AUG	8 AUG TO 23 AUG	24 AUG TO 12 SEP	13 SEP TO 24 SEP
FRIS RET SUN	REF MTF	MXF								
SATS RET MON	REF MTS	MXS								
No. OF DAYS	10	17	10 17	10 17	10 17	10 17	10 17	10 17	10 17	10 17
4/6 PERSONS PER TENT			64 79	79 94	89 109	99 124	124 149	114 139	99 124	89 109
2/3 PERSONS PER TENT			70 91	85 106	95 121	105 136	130 161	120 151	105 136	95 121

CHILD AGED 2-11 DEDUCT £40 PER HOLIDAY MAY, JUNE & SEP DEPS. £30 JULY & AUG DEPS.

DEPARTURE SUPPLEMENTS		DEP TIME	RET TIME	DEPARTURE SUPPLEMENTS		DEP TIME	RET TIME	DEPARTURE SUPPLEMENTS		DEP TIME	RET TIME
BIRMINGHAM	£7.00	0800	2015	LEEDS	£11.50	0700	2200	NOTTINGHAM	£9.50	0700	2335
BRADFORD	£12.00	0630	2230	LEICESTER	£8.00	0745	2045	PLYMOUTH	£13.50	0700	2315
BRISTOL	£10.00	0830	2030	LONDON	No. Supp	1130	1700	PORTSMOUTH	£9.50	0800	2130
CARDIFF	£10.00	0700	2200	MANCHESTER	£11.00	0700	2115	SHEFFIELD	£11.00	0720	2210
COVENTRY	£8.00	0815	2215	NORWICH	£8.00	0720	2230	SOUTHAMPTON	£8.00	0815	2130
								SWANSEA	£12.00	0640	2325

Prices are per person from London. Children under 2 free.

Exercise 130

Read the brochure panel carefully.

a) If you and a friend went on this camping holiday from the 8th to 18th August it would cost you £120.00 each.
   If you went in early May how much would you pay?

b) How much extra would you pay to depart from Nottingham?

c) If you departed on a Friday, on which day would you return?

d) Using the information above, work with a partner. Imagine that you are in a travel agent's shop. Ask for details about departures from Coventry.

Exercise 131

Go back to your holiday brochures and the resort or activity which you like best.
Answer these questions about it:

a) What is your chosen departure date?
b) When would you return home?
c) What is the name of your chosen hotel, apartment, caravan or camping site?
d) In which country is it situated?
e) What will be the basic cost?
f) Do you think there will be any extra costs?

Exercise 132

Read the extract from a holiday advertisement and then talk about the words ringed. Why has the advertiser chosen these words? What are they meant to tell you?

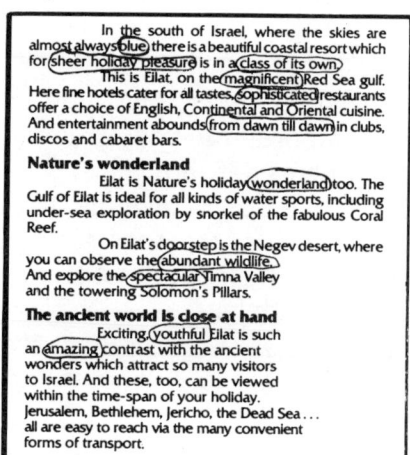

In the south of Israel, where the skies are almost always blue there is a beautiful coastal resort which for sheer holiday pleasure is in a class of its own.
This is Eilat, on the magnificent Red Sea gulf. Here fine hotels cater for all tastes. Sophisticated restaurants offer a choice of English, Continental and Oriental cuisine. And entertainment abounds from dawn till dawn in clubs, discos and cabaret bars.

Nature's wonderland
Eilat is Nature's holiday wonderland too. The Gulf of Eilat is ideal for all kinds of water sports, including under-sea exploration by snorkel of the fabulous Coral Reef.
On Eilat's doorstep is the Negev desert, where you can observe the abundant wildlife. And explore the spectacular Timna Valley and the towering Solomon's Pillars.

The ancient world is close at hand
Exciting, youthful Eilat is such an amazing contrast with the ancient wonders which attract so many visitors to Israel. And these, too, can be viewed within the time-span of your holiday. Jerusalem, Bethlehem, Jericho, the Dead Sea... all are easy to reach via the many convenient forms of transport.

Exercise 133

Read the following holiday brochure information about Sweden, then use it to prepare and give a talk about the attractions of a holiday in Sweden.

Set out to discover Sweden; see the uncrowded, unhurried, unspoilt cities and countryside. Find miles of silver sands, rocky, exciting coastlines, hundreds of lakes, and miles of forest full of wildlife. It is so easy, most Swedes speak English, there are no language problems.

You can choose from a wide selection of places and types of holiday; splendid hotels, self-catering, camping or touring holidays you will never forget.

Exercise 134

Work with a partner. Imagine that one of you is the holiday-maker and the other the travel agent. Answer these questions.

a) Which ferry port is nearest to Piriac?
b) How long does it take to disembark?
c) How long will it take to drive from the ferry port to Piriac?

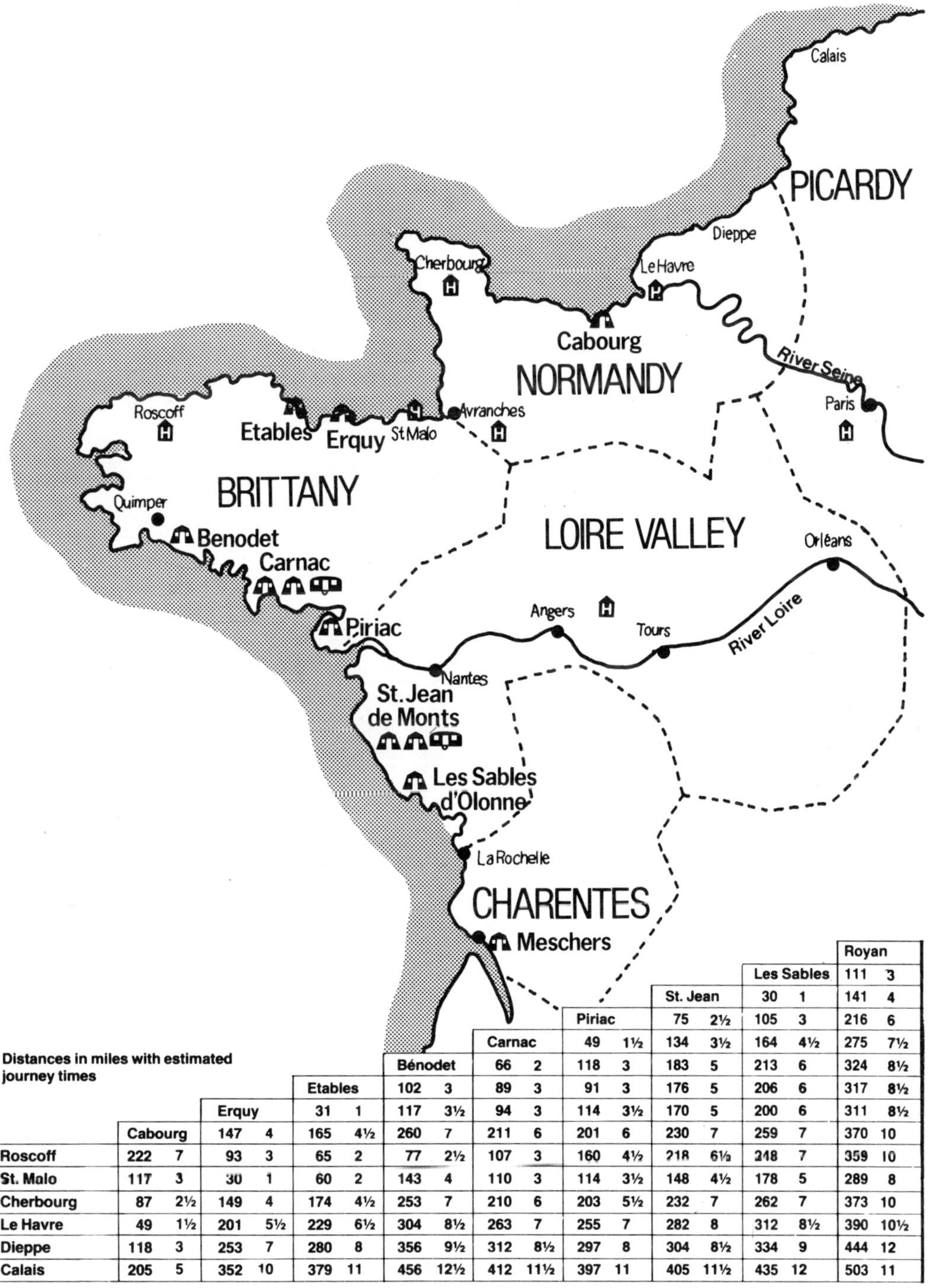

[Map of north-western France showing regions PICARDY, NORMANDY, BRITTANY, LOIRE VALLEY and CHARENTES, with towns including Calais, Dieppe, Le Havre, Cherbourg, Cabourg, Avranches, St Malo, Etables, Erquy, Roscoff, Quimper, Bénodet, Carnac, Piriac, Nantes, Angers, Tours, Orléans, Paris, St. Jean de Monts, Les Sables d'Olonne, La Rochelle, Meschers. Rivers Seine and Loire are marked.]

Distances in miles with estimated journey times

	Cabourg		Erquy		Etables		Bénodet		Carnac		Piriac		St. Jean		Les Sables		Royan	
Royan																		
Les Sables																	111	3
St. Jean															30	1	141	4
Piriac													75	2½	105	3	216	6
Carnac											49	1½	134	3½	164	4½	275	7½
Bénodet									66	2	118	3	183	5	213	6	324	8½
Etables							102	3	89	3	91	3	176	5	206	6	317	8½
Erquy					31	1	117	3½	94	3	114	3½	170	5	200	6	311	8½
Cabourg			147	4	165	4½	260	7	211	6	201	6	230	7	259	7	370	10
Roscoff	222	7	93	3	65	2	77	2½	107	3	160	4½	218	6½	248	7	359	10
St. Malo	117	3	30	1	60	2	143	4	110	3	114	3½	148	4½	178	5	289	8
Cherbourg	87	2½	149	4	174	4½	253	7	210	6	203	5½	232	7	262	7	373	10
Le Havre	49	1½	201	5½	229	6½	304	8½	263	7	255	7	282	8	312	8½	390	10½
Dieppe	118	3	253	7	280	8	356	9½	312	8½	297	8	304	8½	334	9	444	12
Calais	205	5	352	10	379	11	456	12½	412	11½	397	11	405	11½	435	12	503	11

Included in the mileage chart are estimates of the actual driving times in hours. Please remember to add time for stops and up to half an hour for disembarkation. The time between Calais and Royan is based on using the Paris to Poitiers Autoroute (Toll).

To travel abroad you will need a passport. You should apply for a passport on the proper form, at least four weeks before your holiday. It is better to apply as soon as possible.

Here are some notes from an Application for a British Visitor's passport. Read them carefully.

Visitor's Passport

What documents are needed
One of the documents listed below is needed for **each** person to be included on the passport (photographic copies are not acceptable).
a A birth certificate or adoption certificate showing full names issued in the United Kingdom or abroad by a United Kingdom authority;
b A National Health Service Medical Card in your present name;
c A DHSS Retirement Pension Book or Pension Card BR464 in your present name;
d An uncancelled Standard British Passport or British Visitor's Passport in your present name (or husband's/wife's if included on it).

Photographs
2 recent, identical photographs size 50mm x 38mm (2″ by 1½″) of yourself (and 2 of your wife/husband if she/he is to be included on the passport). The photographs should be taken full face without a hat. Photographs are not required for an included child.

How much does it cost?
£7.50
£11.25 if wife/husband is to be included.

How and where do I get the passport?
By taking your completed application form, photographs, required documents (see above) and fee, **in person** (if your wife/husband is to be on the passport she/he must go with you. A child for whom a separate Visitor's Passport is required must also go with you) to:

in			(Monday to Friday only)
	England Wales Scotland	A Main Post Office ,, ,,	
in	Northern Ireland	Passport Office Hampton House 47-53 High Street Belfast BT1 2QS	(Tel 232371)
in	Jersey	Passport Office	St Helier (Tel 25377)
in	Guernsey	,,	St Peter Port (Tel 26911)
in	Isle of Man	,,	Douglas (Tel 26262)

Visitor's passports are not obtainable from mainland Passport Offices in Glasgow, Liverpool, London, Newport or Peterborough.

Wife/Husband included on the passport
can **only** use it when they are travelling with the holder

Children on the passport
Children can **only** be included on a parent's (or step-parent's/adoptive parent's, brother's or sister's passport and then **only** until they are 16 years old. When they are 16 or over, they must have their own passport. They cannot travel on their own using a passport in which they are only included. Children under 8 cannot have their own Visitor's Passport.

Amendments to the passport
You cannot have the passport altered in any way after it has been issued e.g. you cannot have your wife/husband/child added to it.

Post-dated passports
You cannot have a Visitor's passport post-dated or issued in a future married name for your use immediately after your marriage.

Care of passports
Your passport is an important document. If you lose it you should inform the Police and the Passport Office, Glasgow. If you are abroad you should inform the nearest British Consulate or High Commission.

Exercise 135

a) Which documents are needed to send with your application?
b) What else do you need to send?
c) Where should you send your completed application?
d) From which Passport Office can you not get a British Visitor's passport?
e) May a wife travelling alone use a joint passport?
f) How old must you be to have a visitor's passport?
g) Who should you tell if you lose your passport?
h) Draw and address an envelope to your Passport Office.

Here is John Smith's application form, see how he has completed it.

Passport holder (person whose name will appear on passport)

Please write clearly in ink using CAPITAL LETTERS

Mr. Mrs. Miss., Ms or title	MR
Surname	SMITH
Forename(s) or Christian name(s)	JOHN
Maiden surname (if any)	—
Date of birth	3.7.68 — Age 17
Town of birth	HULL — Country of birth ENGLAND
Present address in the United Kingdom	32 DUBLIN ROAD, HULL, NORTH HUMBERSIDE — Postcode HU 17 1XZ
Height in metres (see conversion table right)	1·88
Visible distinguishing marks (if any)	NONE

The measurement of height
Height in passports is now shown in metric units. A conversion table follows

feet	inches	metres	feet	inches	metres
4	0	1.22	5	3	1.60
4	1	1.24	5	4	1.63
4	2	1.27	5	5	1.65
4	3	1.30	5	6	1.68
4	4	1.32	5	7	1.70
4	5	1.35	5	8	1.73
4	6	1.37	5	9	1.75
4	7	1.40	5	10	1.78
4	8	1.42	5	11	1.80
4	9	1.45	6	0	1.83
4	10	1.47	6	1	1.85
4	11	1.50	6	2	1.88
5	0	1.52	6	3	1.90
5	1	1.55	6	4	1.93
5	2	1.57	6	5	1.96

Exercise 136

Write out your personal details in the same way that John has done on his application form.

People who travel abroad cannot use English money. They need to use the right kind of foreign money or currency. Most holiday-makers take travellers' cheques to exchange for foreign currency.

English pounds have been done for you.

Austria	Schillings
Belgium	Belgian Francs
France	Francs
Germany	Deutschmarks
Greece	Drachmas
Italy	Lira
Netherlands	Guilders
Spain	Pesetas
Switzerland	Swiss Francs

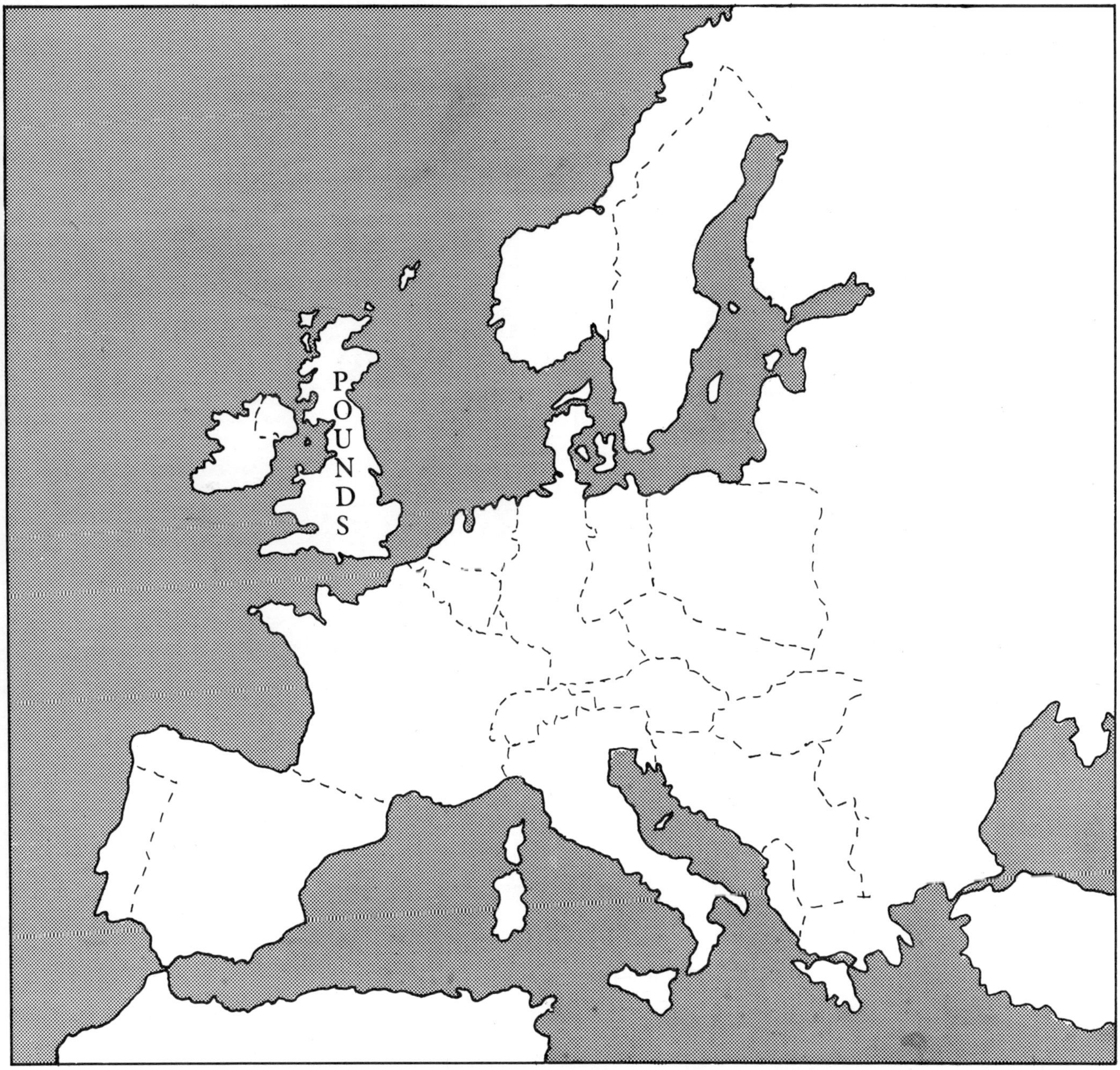

Exercise 137

Copy this map of Europe. Write each of the following currencies in the correct space on the map.

When you are away on holiday, family and friends at home like to receive a postcard.

Exercise 138

Talk about the reasons why people like to receive postcards.

Exercise 139

Using an atlas and a holiday brochure collect details about a resort, the weather and things of interest and an hotel.

a)   Talk about the things which parents or friends might like to know about your journey and holiday
b)   Draw a postcard like the one below, address it to your parents or to a friend.
c)   Write postcard messages for i) parents, ii) friends.

Mrs A. Smith,
32 Dublin Road,
Hull,
North Humberside.
HU17 1XZ
ENGLAND

When you return home from your holiday, you will want those superb photographs developed and printed as soon as possible.

Exercise 140

Read the film envelope on the right, then answer these questions about it:

a)   If your camera uses 110/24 film, how much will:
regular prints cost?
30% bigger prints cost?
b)   What size are 30% bigger prints?
c)   To whom should a cheque or P.O. be made payable?
d)   What is the cost of a duplicate set of prints?

e)   How much postage will you need to pay?
f)   How much does post and packing cost?
g)   Talk about the meaning of 'No Quibble Guarantee'. What does it mean?

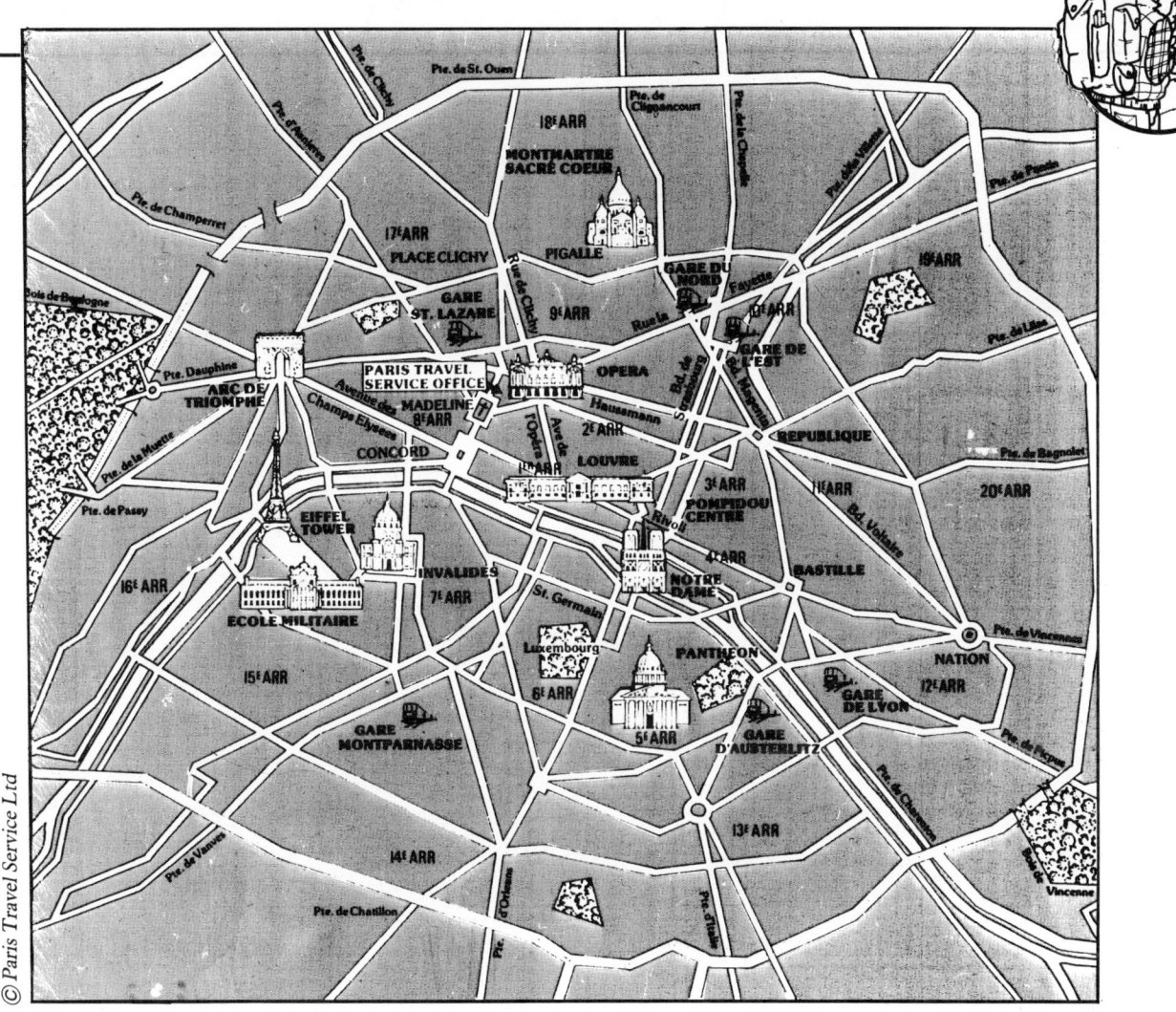

© Paris Travel Service Ltd

For a great number of young people the school trip to Paris, or some channel port is their first experience of travel abroad. France is just a short sea journey away, it does not take long on a modern high speed ferry.

Exercise 141

Imagine that you have arrived in Paris with a party of young people. Your hotel is in the Rue la Fayette close to the Gare du Nord.

Look closely at the map of Paris, then complete these tasks.

a) You are to meet friends at Notre Dame, how would you walk there from your hotel?
b) Explain to a friend how to get from the Ecole Militaire to Notre Dame.
c) Leave a note at the hotel for any latecomers, explain your plans and give some written instructions about finding you.

Exercise 142

As a part of your outing you must take a turn at being guide for the day. This involves planning the day's outings, deciding on the route to walk, and giving instructions to each member of the group. Sometimes instructions are written, often they are given orally.

a) Give written instructions for walking from the Gare du Nord to the Louvre via the Arc De Triomphe, the Eiffel Tower and Invalides.
b) Exlain to your group the following details of a walking trip around Paris. You will leave the Opera to visit the Madeleine, Champs Elysees, Statue of Liberty, the Place de la Concorde, finishing up at the Eiffel Tower.

Travel Insurance is a good idea. You can insure yourself and your party before travelling abroad. The policy below is designed to cover you for almost anything that could happen on a holiday: illness, accident, loss or delays. Even if you have to cancel your holiday you can claim the cost.

Draw this form and complete it in the names of Mr J.O. Brown, Mrs E.S. Brown, and their two children Alice and Elizabeth. They will be flying to Spain for a fourteen-day holiday.

Premium Rates

*Areas	Up to 5 days		6-10 days		11-18 days		19-31 days		Each Additional Week or Part Up To 3 Months
	Adult	Child	Adult	Child	Adult	Child	Adult	Child	Adult Child — Available on Request
1. UK, and The Isle of Man	£ 6.00	£ 4.50	£ 6.00	£ 4.50	£ 7.50	£ 5.60	£10.00	£ 7.50	
2. The Channel Islands, Republic of Ireland, Europe, Mediterranean Islands, Morocco, Algeria, Tunisia, Libya, Egypt, Israel, Lebanon, Jordan, Syria, Turkey, Madeira and Canary Isles.	£ 7.50	5.60	£10.00	£ 7.50	£11.00	£ 8.25	£15.00	£11.25	£ 3.50 £ 2.60

APPLICATION FORM

Surname and initials of insured persons	Premium per person
1	
2	
3	
4	
5	

Total [ ]

Areas: see premium rates and tick box   1 [ ] 2 [ ]

Date of Departure   Date of Return

Address of first insured person

_____

_____

_____

Post Code   Telephone

I enclose a cheque/P.O. for the total premium
Please debit my credit card account (tick box)   [ ]
Credit card number _____
Signature _____ Date _____

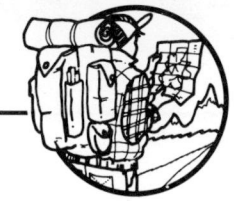

Holiday booking forms like the one below can be very complicated. There are also a lot of entries to make or boxes to tick.

Exercise 144

Complete this form. remember, if you make mistakes you may not get the holiday you want.

Make the booking for a party comprising: you and two friends wishing to travel to a campsite in Menton via the Dover/Calais ferry, on August 1st and back on the 22nd. You will be travelling in a Vauxhall Chevette, registration CRH747 X. The most suitable ferries for you are at 0600 hours going and 1800 hours on your return. It will take two days to drive from Calais to Menton.

Your Party

Title	Initials	Surname	Age

Home address of Party Leader

_____

_____

Postcode _____

Telephone _____

Your camp-sites	T/c	Date	
		From	**To**

Travel/Ferries Outward

Port	Departure	Time	Date
	Homeward		

Car/Make	Model	Reg.No.

I agree to pay a deposit of 10% on the receipt of your invoice and the balance 14 days before departure.

Signed _____ Date _____

Paris excursions by day

1. HISTORIC PARIS £8.50
Daily at 9.15 a.m. (2½hrs)
Starting at the Opéra this instructive tour visits the Marais, Places des Victoires, La Bastille, the Ile de la Cité representing the heart of Paris with the Palais de Justice, Conciergerie and Notre Dame Cathedral, thence to the Left Bank passing the Boulevard St. Michel, the Sorbonne University and the Luxembourg Gardens. You will also see the Panthéon, the Marché aux fleurs and St. Germain des Prés as well as the Louvre, etc. The tour takes you by the Louvre and the Luxembourg Gardens and a detailed visit to Notre Dame Cathedral.

2. MONTMARTRE AND WESTERN PARIS £8.50
Daily at 1.45 p.m. (2½hrs)
This very interesting tour starts at the Place de l'Opéra (the Piccadilly Circus of Paris) and visits the Madeleine, Champs Elysées, Statue of Liberty, the Place de la Concorde, the Eiffel Tower and the Arc de Triomphe, Palais de Chaillot, Alexandre III Bridge, Montmartre, Place du Tertre and the magnificent Sacré Coeur Basilica.

3. FONTAINEBLEAU AND BARBIZON £15.50
Wednesday, Friday 1.45 p.m. and Sunday 8.45 a.m. (½ day)
This famous Palace in the beautiful forest of Fontainebleau, at one time the favourite meeting place of the Royal Hunt, has been enriched with paintings, tapestries and furnishings by ten centuries of French Kings, whilst the artistic centre of Barbizon was the home of many French painters and writers.

4. VERSAILLES £11.00
Afternoon (except Sunday and Monday) at 1.45 p.m.
(From Easter to October, also mornings daily at 9.15 a.m. except Mondays)
A delightful half day drive to the world famous Palace which combines the classicism of the 17th century with the elegance and baroque style of the 18th century. Three famous kings of France lived here; Louis XIV who originally built the Palace, his successor Louis XV and finally, the ill-fated Louis XVI who, with his Queen Marie Antoinette, was overtaken by the great revolution. A visit to the richly decorated interior is included as well as a tour of the world famous gardens.

5. BATEAUX MOUCHES £1.90
(Seine river sightseeing boats)
Afternoon cruises (1 hour)
3.00 p.m. daily
These well-known boats are large and comfortable with air-conditioning and perspex enclosed decks (retractable) and passengers may view the sights in comfort in all weathers. There is a good bar and tea lounges on board, also with visual and broadcast commentary in several languages. This afternoon cruise (1 hour approximately) gives entirely new and unforgettable views of the city passing many famous bridges and with unique views of the Eiffel Tower, the Louvre, Ile de la Cité, Notre Dame, etc.

6. TUESDAY SPECIAL £18.80
Every Tuesday (6 hours)
All year round 9.00 a.m.
A special whole day sightseeing tour of Paris including lunch, personally guided by a Paris Travel Service Hostess and including visits to the Place de la Concorde and up the impressive Champs Elysées to the Arc de Triomphe. From the Place du Trocadero see the Eiffel Tower and in the distance the gardens of the Champs de Mars then up into Montmartre and views over Paris from the steps of the magnificent Sacre Coeur. After lunch down to the Seine, past the Louvre to Notre Dame Cathedral on the Ile de la Cité and back via the Latin Quarter to the Opera. Lunch and wine tasting visit included in price.

© *Paris Travel Service Ltd*

As in any large city, there is a lot for the sightseer to do in Paris. There are many very historic, and romantic places to visit. It would be impossible to visit them all, on foot, in only a few days; so most people take a trip.

Read the details of the 'Paris excursions by day' very carefully. You will need some information about the excursions to complete these tasks.

Exercise 145

You are in Paris for four days and intend to have one coach trip each day. You want to see as much as you can as cheaply as you can.

a) Which four trips would you choose?
b) Explain how these four trips fit your plans.

Exercise 146

Write a postcard home to your parents or to a friend, tell them all about one of your coach trips. Mention the things you have seen and the places which you have visited.

Exercise 147

The mixed-up words below can all be found on the map of Paris or in the 'Paris excursions by day'. Find the place names in these mixed-up words and write them down.

e.g. **a rope** when sorted out is the Opera.

tenomratm
ableafutnion
saiversell
texchesbuomaua
sedilavni

revolu
stilbale
quilperbue
nolyageerd
ontheap

Exercise 148

Write a story about a journey abroad. You may use some of the information from this chapter to provide a framework. Try to imagine some of the problems which you might have and the many interesting experiences you may undergo.

Remember
★ Write in proper sentences.
★ Change to a new paragraph for a new topic.

Wordsearch

See if you can find all of these words in the wordsearch below:

Entertainment	Tour
Enjoyment	Booking
Mileage	Camping
Passport	Deposit
Holiday	Document
Basic	Remittance
Apartment	Disembark
Collection	Brochure
Operator	Distance
Weather	Postcard
Expensive	Resort
Agent	Extra
Photograph	Excitement
Aeroplane	Visitor
Ferry	Travel

A	J	B	P	E	D	F	F	N	D	Y	P	L	O	W	Q	B	V	S
E	H	X	F	D	R	P	A	S	S	P	O	R	T	L	T	T	M	L
R	R	N	N	L	A	H	X	G	V	R	O	T	I	S	I	V	L	W
O	J	U	B	U	C	O	L	L	E	C	T	I	O	N	S	T	O	Q
P	S	R	H	F	T	T	U	X	N	N	G	T	S	K	O	B	V	C
L	S	V	O	C	S	O	V	A	T	D	T	O	U	R	P	V	J	O
A	M	B	L	C	O	G	R	F	E	N	J	O	Y	M	E	N	T	X
N	H	F	I	Y	P	R	F	P	R	X	H	P	M	A	D	C	H	N
E	V	J	D	S	E	A	B	K	T	E	C	A	M	P	I	N	G	N
S	R	X	A	N	R	P	A	D	A	R	M	I	L	E	A	G	E	W
O	F	H	Y	U	A	H	S	O	I	P	A	I	T	V	X	Y	V	T
L	T	I	L	Q	T	A	I	C	N	S	A	V	T	E	B	T	D	S
G	N	I	K	O	O	B	C	U	M	H	E	R	E	T	M	J	R	X
T	R	O	S	E	R	N	M	M	E	L	E	M	T	L	A	E	H	A
E	V	I	S	N	E	P	X	E	N	C	A	C	B	M	F	N	N	E
W	W	J	A	P	P	M	E	N	T	R	E	H	T	A	E	W	C	T
U	O	I	F	B	D	I	S	T	A	N	C	E	Q	F	R	N	X	E
L	S	R	P	W	V	J	R	W	C	N	P	H	U	W	R	K	T	F
F	I	C	U	Q	D	O	S	D	G	G	K	W	W	O	Y	H	K	A